THE ODES OF SOLOMON
Mystical Songs from the Time of Jesus

Born in 1944, John Davidson has had a lifelong interest in mysticism. Graduating in 1966 from Cambridge University with an honours degree in natural sciences, he worked for seventeen years at the University's Department of Applied Mathematics and Theoretical Physics.

In 1984, he left the University to pursue independent interests, and since then has written a number of books, including a series on science and mysticism. The present book is the sixth in a series on Christian origins, following on from his ground-breaking work, *The Gospel of Jesus: In Search of His Original Teachings.*

BY THE SAME AUTHOR

On Science and Mysticism

Subtle Energy (1987)
The Web of Life (1988)
The Secret of the Creative Vacuum (1989)
Natural Creation and the Formative Mind (1991)
Natural Creation or Natural Selection? (1992)

On Christian Origins

The Robe of Glory (1992)
The Gospel of Jesus (1995, revised 2004)
The Prodigal Soul (2004)
The Divine Romance (2004)
The Song of Songs (2004)

THE ODES OF SOLOMON

Mystical Songs from the Time of Jesus

John Davidson

cb

CLEAR BOOKS

First published in Great Britain in 2004 by
Clear Press Limited,
Unit 136, 3 Edgar Buildings
George Street, Bath BA1 2FJ
www.clearpress.co.uk

Designed by Rick Fry and John Davidson
Typeset by John Davidson
Cover design by Jerry Goldie
Printed in India by Ajanta Offset

British Library Cataloguing in
Publication data available

Library of Congress Cataloging in
Publication data available

ISBN 1–904555–06–3

DEDICATION

To my Helper

My joy is the Lord, and my course is to Him:
this my path is beautiful.
For I have a Helper to the Lord.
He made himself known to me,
without grudging, in his generosity:
For in his kindness,
he set aside his majesty.
He became like me,
in order that I might accept him.
Odes of Solomon *7:2–6*

ACKNOWLEDGEMENTS

This book could not have been written without the prior work of a number of scholars. The *Odes* themselves are a carefully collated rendering of the translations made by J.R. Harris (*The Odes and Psalms of Solomon;* Cambridge University Press, Cambridge, 1911), J.H. Bernard (*The Odes of Solomon;* Cambridge University Press, Cambridge, 1912), J.R. Harris and A. Mingana (*The Odes and Psalms of Solomon,* 2 vols.; Longmans, Green and Co., London, 1920), J.H. Charlesworth (*The Odes of Solomon;* Oxford University Press, Oxford, 1973; and "The Odes of Solomon" in *The Old Testament Pseudo-epigrapha,* 2 vols., ed. J.H. Charlesworth; Darton, Longman and Todd, London, 1983) and J.A. Emerton ("The Odes of Solomon", in *The Apocryphal Old Testament,* ed. H.E.D. Sparks; Oxford University Press, Oxford, 1985).

Passages from the Manichaean psalms and the Mandaean Prayer Book are modernized adaptations of the original translations, respectively, of C.R.C. Allberry (*A Manichaean Psalm Book,* Part II; Kohlhammer, Stuttgart, 1938) and E.S. Drower (*The Canonical Prayerbook of the Mandaeans;* E.J. Brill, Leiden, 1959).

Excerpts from the *Acts of Thomas* are modernizations and often collations of the translations of M.R. James (in *The Apocryphal New Testament;* Oxford University Press, Oxford, 1989 [1924]) and W.R. Wright (in *The Apocryphal Acts of the Apostles;* Williams and Norgate, Edinburgh, 1871).

Extracts from the *Thanksgiving Hymns* among the Dead Sea

Scrolls are from the translations of Geza Vermes (*The Complete Dead Sea Scrolls in English;* Penguin, London, 1998), rendered into modern English.

Biblical passages are drawn mostly from the *Authorized King James Version, The Jerusalem Bible* and *The New Jerusalem Bible.* Excerpts from *The Jerusalem Bible,* published and copyright 1966, 1967 and 1968 by Doubleday (USA & Canada), a division of Random House Inc., and by Darton, Longman & Todd (rest of the world) are reprinted by permission of the publishers.

The precise sources of these and other extracts are provided in the relevant notes and references.

Thanks are also due to a number of friends who have been through the manuscript making various valuable suggestions, in particular, Bridget Cuffolo, Luke Hardy, Penny Norris, Cindy Rawlinson, Geoff Wade and Elwanda Whitten.

CONTENTS

Contents

INTRODUCTION

Sorting one day through a pile of miscellaneous manuscripts lying in a corner of his office, the early twentieth-century biblical scholar, Rendel Harris, realized that he unknowingly had in his possession an almost complete text of the previously lost, *Odes of Solomon*. His first annotated edition of the original text, together with an English translation, was subsequently published the following year, in 1909. Since that date this collection of beautiful odes has been the subject of a considerable number of scholarly translations and discussions. Harris himself remained intrigued and enchanted with the *Odes*, publishing the last of a number of revised editions of his work in 1920, in collaboration with his friend and fellow scholar, Alphonse Mingana.

The *Odes of Solomon* is a collection of forty-two devotional and mystic poems composed very early in the Christian era, possibly around 100 AD or even earlier, probably in or around the city of Antioch. The original language of composition was almost certainly Greek or Syriac, though a case has also been made for Aramaic, a language akin to Syriac. It is also possible that – like many in those times – the original writer was bilingual, writing the *Odes* in both Greek and Syriac, or supervising their translation from one to the other at an early date.

The *Odes of Solomon* survive in only two main manuscripts, both in Syriac. The first – the one found by Rendel Harris – dates from the fifteenth century, and contains all the odes except 1, 2 and the beginning of 3. The second dates from the tenth century, and is lacking its earlier part, beginning in the middle of *Ode 17*. *Ode 11* is also known from a third-century Greek papyrus. Five other odes (1, 5, 6, 22 and 25) are extant in Coptic, embedded in a well-known gnostic text, the fourth-century *Pistis Sophia*. Pooling these resources, only *Ode 2* and the beginning of *Ode 3* are entirely missing.

Neither of the two Syriac manuscripts are of an early date, and there are differences between these texts, often minor, sometimes significant. One of these two also has occasional verses missing due to the inattention of the scribe. It is certain, therefore, that the extant texts are not entirely as originally penned, and the possibility of significant editing having taken place in some of the odes cannot be ruled out. However, generally speaking, the consistency of the odes suggests that they are largely as the original author intended.

The renderings offered here are new, based upon the work of earlier scholars, notably J.R. Harris (1909, 1911, 1916), J.H. Bernard (1912), J.R. Harris and A. Mingana (1920), J.H. Charlesworth (1973, 1983) and J.A. Emerton (1985). Consideration has also been given to a number of French and German translations and studies. It is noteworthy that the translations subsequent to the original work of Rendel Harris have been considerably influenced by him, as has the present work.

There are a number of places where the translation or interpretation is uncertain. All the scholars involved have acknowledged this. Since the purpose of the present book is to place the *Odes* before the general reader in an enjoyable format, without scholarly notes and commentary, I have had to make a decision, on each occasion, which meaning to go for. While taking account of the technical aspects of the available texts, I have generally opted for the most plausible rendering, given the odist's flow of thought in that particular ode. The division of the *Odes* into stanzas has also been added in the present rendering.

The attribution of the *Odes* to Solomon reflects a common literary device of ancient times. Writings were ascribed to an individual from history or mythology who – it was considered –

represented the ideals and doctrines of that particular text. Traditionally, Solomon represented spiritual and human wisdom, as well as the divine Wisdom or creative Power of God as portrayed in *Proverbs*, the *Wisdom of Solomon*, the *Wisdom of Jesus Ben Sirach* and other literature of the period. Further, the name 'Solomon' (*Shelomo* in Hebrew) has been derived from the Hebrew '*Shalom*', meaning 'peace' or 'rest'. In a spiritual context, 'rest' is a term used throughout Jewish, Christian and other literature for the peace and bliss of eternity. *Ode 26* even speaks of the "Odes of His Rest", probably as a play on the name Solomon, and some scholars have consequently considered the possibility that the *Odes* were originally named the "Odes of His Rest". The ascription of the *Odes* to Solomon indicates, therefore, that their subject matter is spiritual and mystical.

A study of the *Odes* soon reveals that their underlying theme, their choice of metaphors and their linguistic style have much in common with John's gospel. Both writers take the Creative Word or *Logos* to be the fundamental reality of their mystical understanding. In keeping with the times, both exhibit a blend of Jewish and Hellenistic influences. Both are fond of wordplay and *double entendre*, and there are many passages that contain both an outer meaning as well as an inner, mystic meaning. Both also like to echo passages from the Jewish Wisdom literature (*Psalms, Proverbs, Song of Songs, Wisdom of Solomon* and so on). In fact, many of the *Odes* contain allusions and references either to John's gospel, or to the Wisdom literature, or to other biblical texts, many of which have been identified by the various scholarly commentators. There are a number of places where the odist clearly has one of the biblical *Psalms* or some passage from the Wisdom literature in mind, forming his literary inspiration for that passage, or sometimes for an entire ode.

The *Odes* also have affinities with texts such as the hymns found among the Dead Sea Scrolls and the pre-Christian *Psalms of Solomon*, both of which employ a variety of terms when speaking of the Creative Word of God. From the wealth of mystic literature of this kind, stemming from the centuries immediately before and after Jesus, it must be presumed that mystics who taught the path of the Word or *Logos* were active at that time in Palestine and Asia Minor.

There appear to be two main kinds of odes in the collection. There are the simple ones, full of gratitude, love and praise of God; and there are those where the symbolism and imagery is more complex. At times, it is tempting to think that contributions from two authors are present. It would not be without precedent for the *Odes* to contain the work of more than one writer. This is true of the biblical *Psalms* and the book of *Proverbs,* for instance. All the same, there is a unity in the imagery and style that prevails throughout. It is likely that some odes have received the editorial attention of later Christians, explaining why a few are more specifically Christian than others. But in these and other odes it is also evident that the author – as in John's gospel – is trying to indicate the symbolic mystical meaning hidden within the beliefs and myths of early Christian dogma. All in all, then, the general conclusion is that the *Odes* are primarily the work of one writer.

Like John's gospel, the essential theme of the *Odes* is that of salvation and the attainment of immortal life through the primary, creative Power of God, which the odist calls the Word, the Word of Truth, the Word of Knowledge, Wisdom, the Truth, His Thought, Living Water, the Spring or Fountain, His Right Hand, His Name, and by other similar terms and epithets. All of these names are used in earlier biblical and apocryphal literature, as well as later in early Christian and other allied texts. The poet also speaks of a "Helper", whom he equates with the Word, but also identifies as a living human being. This is clearly his Saviour or Master, whom he believes to be an incarnation or manifestation of the Word.

In common with many other mystic writers of the time, direct experience of God is called Knowledge or *Gnosis* of God. The writer also speaks of love, faith, refuge, rest and many other aspects of the devotional, mystic path associated with the Word. All the *Odes* end with the word 'Hallelujah', which means 'praise the Lord', a common expression of the times that has survived the centuries.

The majority of the metaphors and images used in the *Odes* also occur in other literature of the period. Like many poets before and since, one of the odist's most frequent devices is to open a poem with an image, and then to expand upon this image in the remainder of the poem.

At times, it is the devotee who speaks, and at others, the odist assumes the voice of the Messiah or Saviour. In some poems, the two alternate, but the poet has left it up to the reader to figure out who is speaking at any particular point or in any particular ode. Sometimes, it could be either. As in John's gospel, *Isaiah* and many other biblical books, writing in the name of the Saviour, the Word or the Lord himself was a common literary practice of the period.

The meaning of many of the metaphors will usually be clear to the reader, but some will be more obscure than others. The ones that may be the most difficult to appreciate in modern times are those associated with the human body. This imagery is in keeping with the odist's era. The creative Power, for instance, is God's 'Right Hand'; his soul has limbs or 'members' – meaning all parts of his being; souls are also described as God's 'members', being parts of him. The poet's inner attitude of devotion and supplication is described metaphorically as turning his 'face' to God and 'stretching out his arms in prayer'. The soul's fallen condition in this world is described as one of 'sickness'; the soul is 'blind', 'deaf', 'crippled' and 'paralysed', in need of 'healing' and being made to 'stand upright'. The spiritual sustenance that flows from God to the soul is described as milk and honey, the former even being depicted as coming from the 'breasts' of the Lord.

Water, too, is a favourite source of metaphors for the odist. In a hot and arid region of the world, the significance of water to life is readily appreciated. This is the origin of the metaphor, 'Living Water', meaning the creative Power, an expression that can even be traced to Sumerian times of the third millennium

BC. To the poet, the Living Water arises from the 'Lord's Spring'. It flows in 'rivers' or falls as 'dew', watering the plant or flowers of his soul. As a result, he 'blossoms' and 'bears fruit'.

Who the author was is unknown. Whether or not he was a direct disciple of Jesus is difficult to say. Perhaps he was, though it is more likely that he was not. For many of the mystical writers of that period, however, Jesus became a kind of new Solomon, so to speak. Set as the focus or lead character of a story, Jesus rapidly became a traditional vehicle for conveying mystic teachings, as in the many apocryphal Acts, gospels and revelations that appeared in the first few centuries of the Christian era.

It is possible, for example, that even John's gospel was written by the disciple of a mystic other than Jesus, and that the writer only used the gospel story – in his own allegorized way – to convey the mystic teachings of the Creative Word or *Logos*. He also wished to correct some of the misunderstandings that he saw creeping into the nascent Christian religion, and present in the already extant gospels of Mark, Matthew and Luke. As a number of scholars have pointed out, John's gospel is really an extended discourse on its opening verses concerning the Word or *Logos*. Hence, the 'I' who speaks as Jesus is speaking – in the words of the author – as an incarnation of the *Logos*. The majority of the discourses, dialogues and stories were thus not intended to be a historical record of Jesus' actual words and deeds.

Some early Christians even believed that John's gospel had been written by the gnostic Cerinthus (*fl.c.*100 AD), while others thought that it had been written to refute Cerinthus. Whatever the truth of the matter, it seems certain that the writers of both the *Odes* and John's gospel were of the same school of thought. They certainly share a similarity of expression, and both imply in their writings that Jesus had been an incarnation of the *Logos*. But whether Jesus was actually their Master, or they were just using the dawning Christian tradition as a literary vehicle remains open to debate.

Some help is required to appreciate the depths hidden in the ancient imagery of the *Odes*. Yet this needs to be done without intrusion into their intrinsic atmosphere or mood, since the nature of the divine and mystic love expressed in these odes is often of a sublime character. I have experimented with a number of ways of providing this assistance. In the end, I have opted for an introductory summary of the ode's main features, together with a mirror, a parallel or a paraphrase of the ode in modern English. The parallel also contains extracts from allied biblical and other literature of the period. The intention is to illuminate the meaning without the heaviness of definitive explanation.

These parallels should be taken as personal interpretations only, as a help to the reader, not as definitions of the whole meaning. Good poetry such as the *Odes* simultaneously conveys a colourful spectrum of hidden, subtle meanings that vanish as soon as the attempt is made to capture them. Sunshine cannot be caught in a bottle. The *Odes* will also strike each person differently, the impact varying according to their mood and bent of mind. This is the power of poetic imagery, and is another reason why I have avoided direct explanation.

To my mind, therefore, a good way to enjoy the *Odes* might be to read the original, to seek assistance from the summary and parallel to understand any obscurities, and then to reflect upon the meanings and the images as they come into one's mind. I would also suggest proceeding at a slow pace, maybe taking just one or two odes at a time. The *Odes* are too rich to be hurried through.

TO THE READER

Translations of the original *Odes* are placed on the left hand pages with their corresponding parallels on the opposite, right hand pages.

Some odes occupy more than one page. Therefore, to read the odes alone, read the left hand pages only. To read the parallels alone, read the right hand pages only.

Quotations used in the parallels have sometimes been edited to modernize the English or, occasionally, to provide clarification. Any significant editorial clarifications or additions to a translation offered by myself or the original translator have been placed in round brackets, while significant conjectured words or phrases, usually provided by the original translator to fill gaps in an original, defective manuscript, appear in square brackets ([ ]). The use of '?' in such instances indicates that the meaning supplied should be considered conjectural. Where quotations used have been edited for any of the above reasons, this is indicated by the use of *cf.* in the source reference.

The purpose of a translation is to convey meaning. This cannot always be done on a word for word basis, especially when dealing with idiomatic poetry. There are a few places, therefore, where a qualifying adjective has been inserted, or a phrase has been used to convey the meaning of one word. In such instances, in the interests of reader friendliness, the use of round brackets has been avoided.

Ode 1

In beautiful imagery, the poet draws attention to the head as the focus of spiritual energy. Collected together in his spiritual centre, he feels the life currents of God coursing through him. His soul ascends and expands until he finds eternity – the 'crown' of spiritual attainment, of union with God.

The Lord is upon my head like a crown of flowers,
and I shall never be without Him.
A crown of Truth has been plaited for me,
and it has caused Thy shoots to grow within me.
For it is not like a withered crown, which blossoms not:
but Thou art alive upon my head,
and Thou hast blossomed upon me.
Thy fruits are full and perfect:
they are full of Thy salvation.

Hallelujah.

A Crown of Living Flowers

My Lord has plaited me a crown of living flowers. Within my head he dwells, always before my inward eyes. He has woven me a garland of sweet spiritual fragrance. He has made me know his inner presence.

His garland never dies. His flowers of joy and beauty, life and carefreeness, bloom eternally within my soul. And while living here, in this imperfect world, I have harvested the sweet fruit of his perfection and salvation:

> An earthly garland fades,
>   but the Garland of Life is fresh and living.
> The garland of a chosen righteous man is set,
>   and shines on the heads of those
>   who love the Name of Truth.
> The garland is from the world of light
>   and the robe from the everlasting abode.

Mandaean Prayer Book 61; cf. CPM p.51

Ode 2

This ode has not survived!

Ode 3

A simple, moving ode in which the poet says that divine love begins and ends with God. God loves the soul. That is why the soul loves Him. And that love has come about because he has found the "Living One", the "Beloved", the Saviour, and – through love – has become like him.

[In His love do] I clothe myself, ...
and with His love, He loves me.
For I should not have known how to love the Lord
if He had not loved me.
For who is able to know love,
except he who is loved?
I love the Beloved, and my soul loves him,
and where his rest is, there too am I.

And I shall be no stranger at His door,
for there is no begrudging
with the Lord Most High and Merciful.
I have been united to Him,
because the lover has found the Beloved.
And because I love him that is the Son,
I shall become a son.
For he who is joined to him who is immortal,
he, too, will become immortal.
And he who has pleasure in the Living One
will become living.

This is the Spirit of the Lord,
which is without deception,
which teaches the sons of men to know His ways.
Be wise, then, and understanding and vigilant.

Hallelujah.

If He had not Loved me

I have wrapped myself in the mantle of his love. But if he had not shown love to me, I could not have learnt to love him. For who can know the sweet sublimity of love, unless he first be loved? My heart is bound to my Beloved, my soul enraptured by his love. And where in his eternity he rests, there too rest I:

> Herein is love, not that we loved God,
>> but that he loved us....
> We love him, because he first loved us.
>> *1 John 4:10, 19, KJV*

He never treats me as an unknown, knocking at his door. His generosity excels all earthly lords: never will his sense of mercy let him turn me away.

Now that I have found my Master, my soul is swept into the ocean of his love. And since he is a Saviour and a Son of God, I know that soon I too will fully know myself to be his child:

> Behold, what manner of love the Father
>> has bestowed upon us,
>> that we should be called the sons of God.
>> *1 John 3:1; cf. KJV*

For he who meets eternity will himself become eternal. And he who meets a Living One, will find true Life.

He is the Holy Spirit manifested, without self-seeking, guile or mean intent. He teaches men to be like him, to know the One he knows.

Therefore, think well, and watch, and wait.

Ode 4

God is the eternal and immutable One, says the odist. Those who put their trust in Him are never disappointed. He makes Himself known by His Word, His "Seal". Through it, all souls are a part of Him. The poet therefore prays for the sweet grace of the Word to descend upon him like soft rain, reminding the Lord that He has a reputation to maintain as the generous, unregretful giver.

No man can alter Thy Holy Place, O my God,
nor can he move it and put it at another place,
because he has no power over it.
For Thy sanctuary Thou didst arrange
before Thou didst make the regions of creation:
The Ancient One shall not be altered
by those that are younger than Himself.

Thou hast given Thy heart, O Lord,
to Thy faithful ones.
Never wilt Thou fail them,
nor wilt Thou be without fruits:
For one hour of Thy faith,
is more precious than all the days and years.
For who is there that shall put on Thy grace
and be rejected?
For Thy Seal is recognized:
and Thy creatures are known to it,
and Thy heavenly hosts possess it,
and the elect archangels are clothed in it.

Thou hast given us communion with Thyself:
It was not that Thou wast in need of us,
but that we are forever in need of Thee.

No Man can Alter Thy Holy Place

No one can change your eternal, holy dwelling, Lord. For where you live is beyond all time and place. No one has dominion over you, dear Lord, to move you somewhere else. Your holy of holies existed before the worlds began – the Ancient of Days remains unmoved by the youthfulness of time:

> You, Lord of all, are to be glorified –
>   self-existent, unutterable,
>   hidden from all the worlds
>   in the brightness of your glory.
>
> *Acts of Thomas 8; cf. AAA p.245*

You, Lord, are renowned for the softness of your heart. You are always there for those who trust in you. The fruit of your love is always ripe for harvest. To live one moment, one blissful hour, with you is better than a lifetime passed in ignorance, for that is what sustains the soul when death draws near:

> A day in your courts is better than a thousand elsewhere.
> I would rather be a doorkeeper in the house of my God,
>   than live in the tents of wickedness.
>
> *Psalms 84:10, NRSV*

All those who taste your grace will find a place with you. The signature of your Word is universally known. It is written on all things, and is accepted everywhere. Created things only exist by virtue of it; the heavenly realms are permeated by it; and the beings who administer your worlds derive their power from it.

Your gift to us is to be one with you. You have no need of us, but we have eternal need of you:

> It is not that he has need of any creature,
>   but that all the creatures in the world have need of him.
>
> *Testament of Naphtali, OPS p.228*

Sprinkle Thy dews upon us,
and open Thy abundant springs,
which pour forth milk and honey to us.
For there is no regret with Thee,
that Thou shouldest regret anything
that Thou hast promised,
since the end was always known to Thee.

For that which Thou gavest, Thou gavest freely,
so that no longer wilt Thou withdraw,
and then come to them again.
For everything was manifest to Thee, as God,
and ordered from the beginning before Thee.
And Thou, O God, hast made all things.

Hallelujah.

Shower your sweet rain, therefore; let the fountains of your Living Water flow; pour out for us the spiritual drink for which we yearn:

> And he shall be to you a fountain
> 　springing up in this thirsty land;
> And a chamber full of food
> 　in this place of them that hunger;
> And a rest unto your souls.
>
> *Acts of Thomas 37, ANT p.383*

Nothing hinders your generosity, my Lord, for what you have promised has already been accomplished. You have always known the ending of the story.

　Whatever you have given has been freely given. No more will you play the game of hide and seek with those whom you have bound securely to yourself. For all of time – the past, the present and the future – is known to you, and has been so from the start. For everything is your creation:

> He is without beginning and without end....
> He has not had anyone who initiated his own existence.
> Thus, he is himself unchanged,
> 　and no one else can remove him from his existence....
> Nor is it possible for anyone else to change him
> 　into a different form or to reduce him,
> 　or alter him or diminish him ...
> 　who is the unalterable, immutable One,
> 　with immutability clothing him.
>
> *Tripartite Tractate 52, NHS22 pp.192–95*

Ode 5

The poet expresses his trust and faith in God's love, and in the Lord's ability to save him from the enemies of his soul – his human imperfections. Even if the world should come to an end, he says, he will remain unconcerned, because he has found sanctuary with the eternal One.

I give thanks to Thee, O Lord,
because I love Thee.
O Most High, do not forsake me,
for Thou art my hope.
Freely have I received Thy grace:
now I will live by it.

My persecutors will come, but they will not see me:
a cloud of darkness will fall upon their eyes,
and an air of deep gloom
will bring darkness upon them.
And they will have no light to see,
by which they could lay hold of me.
May their counsel become thick darkness;
And what they have cunningly devised:
may it recoil upon their own heads.
For they devised a counsel,
but it did not succeed.
(And they were overcome,
though they were powerful).
And they prepared themselves for evil,
but were found to be impotent.

Because I Love Thee

I thank you, dear Lord, for the love that you have given me. Never withdraw this love, for I only trust in you. You have surrounded me with the gift of grace, and it has become my stronghold and my dwelling:

> I thank you with all my heart, Lord my God,
>   I will glorify your name forever:
> Your love for me has been so great.
>
> *Psalms 86:12–13; cf. JB, NJB*

Now the enemies of my soul – my human imperfections and the forces that detain me here – can lay no hold on me. They are like an army upon whom a thick veil has fallen, so that they cannot see me.

The pitfalls they devise to trap my soul are certainly ingenious: may they fall into their own traps and leave me to go free! The network of illusion that they weave is subtle, yet I see through it. They are ready to drag me down, but they have lost their power:

> In your loving kindness, answer me, Yahweh,
>   in your great tenderness, turn to me;
> Do not hide your face from your servant:
>   quick, I am in trouble, answer me;
> Come to my side, redeem me,
>   from so many enemies, ransom me.
>
> You well know the insults I endure,
>   every one of my oppressors is known to you;
> The insults have broken my heart,
>   my shame and disgrace are past cure.
>
> *Psalms 69:16–20; cf. JB, NJB*

For my hope is in the Lord,
and I shall not fear.
And because the Lord is my salvation,
I shall not be concerned.
He is like a crown upon my head,
and I shall not be disturbed.
Even if everything should be shaken,
I shall stand firm.
And if all things visible were to be dissolved,
I shall not die:
Because the Lord is with me,
and I am with Him.

Hallelujah.

My trust is in God, and this world is no concern of mine:

> Even though I walk
>   through the valley of the shadow of death,
>   I will fear no evil.
> For you are with me.
>
> *Psalms 23:4; cf. KJV*

The Lord has delivered me from all negative forces. He has crowned me with Life, and lives within me. Though the entire creation were to shake on its foundation, I would not be moved. Were it to be dissolved today, I would live on eternally. For my God dwells in me, and I in him.

Ode 6

An ode that speaks of the power of the Creative Word. It is the force that inspires the soul through the sound of its heavenly music, bringing vitality to mind and body. It is the means by which God can be known. It is a powerful torrent that overcomes all imperfections and contrary forces. It is the essence of the Saviours – they who hand out this Water of Life to the spiritually thirsty. Those who recognize such Saviours, says the odist, find their way to eternal life.

As the hand moves over the harp,
and the strings speak –
So speaks the Spirit of the Lord in my members,
and I speak by His love.
For it destroys what is alien,
and everything that is bitter.
And thus it was from the beginning,
and will be to the end;
So that nothing shall oppose Him,
and nothing shall rise up against Him.

The Lord has spread abroad the Knowledge of Himself,
and is zealous that those things should be known,
which by His grace have been given to us.
And He has given us the praise of His Name:
so that our spirits may worship His Holy Spirit.

The Harp of God

As the hand of the harpist plays a harp, and fine melodies issue from its strings, so does the Holy Spirit play upon the strings of my being, and his love inspire my words. For his Spirit uproots all imperfections and purifies the heart, so that it sings only the sweetest songs. And so it has always been, right from the start; for nothing can hinder the passage of his love:

> Love no flood can quench,
>> no torrents drown.
>> *Song of Songs 8:7, NJB*

God has made himself accessible, and is anxious that whatever has been so generously given to us should be shared by many:

> The earth shall be filled
>> with the Knowledge of the glory of God,
>> as the waters cover the sea.
>> *Habakkuk 2:14, KJV*

To this end, he has revealed his hidden Name, and showed us how to worship in the Spirit:

> Blessed forever be his glorious Name,
>> may the whole world be filled with his glory.
>> *Psalms 72:19, JB*

For there went forth a Stream,
and it became a river, great and broad;
And it carried away and shattered everything,
and it brought Water
to the temple (of the body?).
And the barriers that were built by men
were unable to restrain it,
nor the art of them whose business it is to restrain it.
And it spread over the surface of all the earth,
and filled everything.
And all the thirsty upon earth were given to drink of it,
and their thirst was relieved and quenched.
For from the Most High was the draught given.

Blessed, therefore, are the Ministers of that Drink,
those who have been entrusted with His Water.
They have assuaged parched lips,
and have awakened the will that was paralysed.
And souls that were close to expiring,
they have brought back from the brink of death.
And limbs that were crooked,
they have been straightened and set up.
They gave strength for feebleness,
and light to the eyes:
For they all recognized them (the Ministers) as the Lord,
and thus gained life by the Living Water of eternity.

Hallelujah.

No barriers can stand before this Power. It is an outpouring, an emanation from the divine Source, bringing Living Water to the desert of the human temple:

> Do you not know that you are the temple of God,
>   and that the Spirit of God dwells in you?
>
> *1 Corinthians 3:16; cf. KJV*

No human imperfection or suppressive force can hinder it. Neither weakness of the mind, nor confused interpretation of the scriptures, can stand in its way. For the Spirit pervades every corner of creation:

> On the gateway of my heart I wrote, "No thoroughfare".
> Love came laughing by and cried, "I enter everywhere".
>
> *Jami* [1]

By the magic of his ways, all those who yearn to drink receive a cup. His Water wells up from the Fountain of eternity:

> I [thank you, O Lord, for] you have placed me
>   beside a Fountain of Streams in an arid land,
>   and close to a Spring of Waters in a dry land,
>   and beside a watered garden [in a wilderness].
>
> *Thanksgiving Hymns XVI:1–5 (18); cf. CDSS p.278*

Blessed are the faithful Saviours, the Water Bearers who carry this Water from its Source. They satisfy the thirsty heart; they revitalize the spiritual will; they awaken sleeping souls, raising them from the death of the material world. They teach the crooked man the art of walking straight. They exchange divine strength for human weakness; they impart light to the inner eye. When Life from the sacred Waters of eternity wells up in those they help, they recognize that their Saviour has come from God.

Ode 7

An ode with a number of obscurities, but essentially concerning the path to God. The odist first expresses his joy at meeting with the Saviour, he who has humbly stooped down to the human level from the heights of God, to take souls back to Him. To accomplish this, God has made a shining path of divine experience out of His Wisdom, His creative Power. But He has given its administration to the Son (a term for both the creative Power and the Saviour). God, says the poet, is known through the path of the divine Sound or Music that is revealed by His Saviours. It is the mystics who will see God, he says, ending with a description of their blissful and ecstatic state.

Like the rush of indignation against wickedness,
so is the surge of joy towards the Beloved,
yielding fruit without restriction.

My joy is the Lord, and my course is to Him:
this my path is beautiful.
For I have a Helper to the Lord.

He made himself known to me,
without grudging, in his generosity:
For in his kindness,
he set aside his majesty.
He became like me,
in order that I might accept him.
In appearance, he seemed like me,
that I might be clothed in him.
And I did not tremble when I saw him,
because he had compassion for me.
He became like my nature,
that I might come to know him;
And like my form,
that I might not turn away from him.

My Joy is the Lord

As the heart recoils instinctively from evil, so does my soul leap joyfully on seeing my Beloved. He is the gladness of my heart, and my soul pursues the blissful path to him.

He has sent a Saviour to help me find the Lord. And my Saviour found me. Without begrudging the sacrifice he was making, he stooped down from the Height. Making little of his greatness, he came humbly to the human level. He took on man's form to create a bond between us. He became like me, so that I could become like him. And because of his kindness and his understanding, he did not let me feel in awe of him. He made himself like me, to win my confidence and love:

> O what a greatness
>   that came down into bondage!
> O unspeakable liberty
>   brought into slavery by us!
> O incomprehensible glory
>   that is come unto us!

Acts of John 77, ANT p.247

The Father of Knowledge
is the Word of Knowledge.
He who created Wisdom
is wiser than His works.
He who created me when yet I was not,
knew what I would do when I came into being.
Therefore, in his abundant grace,
he (my Helper) had compassion for me,
and permitted me to ask from him,
and to benefit from his sacrifice (of coming here).

For He is the one who is incorruptible,
the perfection of the aeons (inner realms and powers),[2]
and their Father.
He (God) has permitted him (my Helper)
to be revealed to them that are His,
so that they may recognize Him that made them,
and not suppose that they had come into being
of themselves.

Mystic knowledge stems from his creative Wisdom. He who spoke his Word pre-existed his creation. He wrote the story long before I read the lines:

> Before all other things, Wisdom was created.
>
> *Wisdom of Jesus Ben Sirach 1:4, JB*

> Yahweh created me (Wisdom)
>   when his purpose first unfolded,
>   before the oldest of his works.
> From everlasting I was firmly set,
>   from the beginning, before the earth came into being.
> The deep was not, when I was born,
>   there were no springs to gush with water.
> Before the mountains were settled,
>   before the hills, I came to birth; ...

> I was by his side, a master craftsman,
>   delighting him day after day,
>   ever at play in his presence,
>   at play everywhere in his world,
>   delighting to be with the sons of men.
>
> *Proverbs 8:22–31, JB*

From the goodness of his heart, he enabled me to know him, and to ask from him, and to be enriched by him.

The Lord is the Immortal, Perfect One: the Creator of all the heavenly realms. He has made it possible for the glory of his creative Power to be seen and heard by those he chooses, so that they might know their Maker:

> It is he that made us, not we ourselves.
> We are his people,
>   and the sheep of his pasture.
>
> *Psalms 100:3; cf. KJV*

For He has appointed Knowledge (Gnosis) as His Path;
And He has made it (the Path) broad and long,
and established it in complete perfection.
He has placed upon it the footprints of His light,
and it stretches from the beginning to the end.

For it was made by Him,
but it rested in the Son.
And for attaining His salvation,
he (the Son) is in command of everything.
The Most High will be known through His Holy Ones,
who will announce the coming of the Lord
to those that sing songs;
That they may go forth to meet Him,
and may sing to Him with joy,
and with the Harp of many tunes.

He has ordained *gnosis* or experience as the way to travel on this Path. He has fashioned a perfect Highway to himself, a Road traced by his footsteps, radiant with light from its beginning to its end.

He has fashioned this Path, but has given its governance to the Son, the Saviour. The Son takes care of everything: God can be known only through his Holy Ones, his Saviours:

> The Father loves the Son,
>> and has given all things into his hand.
>> *John 3:35; cf. KJV*

To those who hear the divine Music of his Word, the Saviour discloses the Path that leads to him. They rise up, listening to the many melodies of the divine Harp, playing in unstruck, blissful symphony:

The mystics shall come before Him,
and shall be seen before Him.
And they shall praise the Lord for His love,
because He is near and sees all things.

And hatred shall be taken away from the earth
and, along with jealousy, it shall be drowned.
For ignorance has been destroyed,
because the Knowledge of the Lord has come.

They who sing will sing of the grace of the Lord Most High,
and they will bring their songs to Him.
And their hearts
will be like the light of day;
And the music of their voices
like the sublime beauty of the Lord.

And nothing that lives
shall be without divine Knowledge,
nor any that is dumb.
For He has given a mouth to His creation,
to open the voice of its mouth to Him to praise Him.
Confess, therefore, His Power,
and proclaim His grace.

Hallelujah.

And at that Sound divine, my soul –
    that in forgetfulness has lain –
    with a new light does shine.
And unto memory plain,
    of its first splendid origin, attain.

Up through the fields of air it wings,
    till in the highest sphere it dwells.
And a new Music there, it hears,
    Music that wells undying,
    and all other kinds excels.

Luis de León, A Fransisco de Salinas; cf. SSM1 p.264

Those who travel on this Road come into his presence, seeing God and being known by him. They become absorbed in the beauty of his love, and in his closeness and omniscience. All their human imperfections are swept away by an inward joy in God. They are no longer deluded by illusion. They listen to the Song of Sweetness, to the divine Sound of the Spirit. They are like a new dawn, full of pure light, moved by an ineffable joy, their praise a silent symphony of love.

Nothing that exists is lacking of this Essence; none are forever deaf and dumb. They only need to find their voice and hear the heavenly Song. The Divine has conferred this gift on his creation – this means by which he can be known and glorified.

Surrender, therefore, to this Power; abandon yourself to divine devotion; and know the sublime nature of his blessings.

Ode 8

The odist first draws on imagery associated with the spoken word and the Creative Word, which he calls the "Right Hand of the Lord", the "Word of Truth", and the "Name". He exhorts his fellow disciples to take advantage of the help provided by their Saviour and to follow the spiritual path with confidence, for their victory is assured. Then the Saviour speaks, as a personification of the "Word of Truth" and of God Himself, encouraging his disciples to trust him and to accept the spiritual gifts he has to offer. Finally, the odist returns to reiterate the message.

Open, open your hearts to the delightful joy of the Lord,
and let your love overflow from the heart to the lips,
to bring forth fruits to the Lord, living and holy,
and to walk with watchfulness in His light.

Rise up and stand straight,
you who were once brought low.
You, who were silenced, speak,
for your mouth has been opened.
You, who were cast down,
be henceforth lifted up,
for the Righteous One has brought you back to life.

For the Right Hand of the Lord is with you,
and will be your Helper.
And peace was prepared for you,
before your war began.
So hear the Word of Truth,
and receive the Knowledge of the Most High.

Open your Hearts

Open your soul to the sweet delight of the Beloved. Let his love permeate your being from head to toe. Live with an awareness of his presence. Let everything you say or do be an expression of his purity.

You, who once stumbled haltingly in matter, arise and walk upright in the Way of the Spirit. You, whose soul has long been mute, let it now speak loudly in your words and deeds. You, who have been lost in the material world, awake – for your Saviour has come to help you find eternal life.

The divine Creative Word is with you, to guide and help you on the Way:

> I meditate on you all night long,
>> for you have always been my help.
> In the shadow of your wings, I sing for joy;
> My soul clings close to you,
>> your Right Hand supports me.
>
> *Psalms 63:7–8; cf. JB, NJB*

> I am the first, I am also the last.
> My Hand laid the foundations of the earth
>> and my Right Hand spread out the heavens.
>
> *Isaiah 48:12–13, JB*

Eternal rest has been ordained for you as the reward of all your labours. So listen to the heavenly Sound and experience the revelation of his magnificence.

Ode 8

(The Saviour:)

Your flesh will not understand what I am saying to you,
nor your raiment (body) what I reveal to you.
Keep my secret,
you who are kept by it;
Keep my faith,
you who are sustained by it.
And experience my Knowledge,
you who know truly who I am.
Love me with devotion,
you who love.

For I turn not my face away from those that are mine,
because I know them.
Before they came into being,
I knew them;
And on their foreheads,
I set my seal.
I fashioned their members:
my own breasts I prepared for them,
that they might drink my holy milk and live thereby
I took pleasure in them,
and am not ashamed of them.
For they are my workmanship,
and the manifestation of my thoughts.

(The Saviour:) It is not your body that will appreciate this mystery, nor your physical senses that will apprehend this revelation. It is a secret, hidden, inner Road you tread. It will sustain you; but keep silent of its mysteries:

> It is given unto you to know
> the mysteries of the kingdom of heaven.
>
> *Matthew 13:11, KJV*

> (But) you must keep my mysteries for me
> and for the sons of my house.
>
> *Clementine Homilies XIX:20, CH p.305*

Live in the aura of my love, but no one else need know of it. Experience all that I have taught you for yourself, for you have realized who I really am. Surrender to my love, you who love me.

Everything is as it is meant to be. I do not abandon my initiates, for they are my spiritual children. If I have brought them this far, it means I will take them to the end:

> I am the good Shepherd,
> and know my sheep, and am known of mine.
>
> *John 10:14, KJV*

Before they were created, they were known to me, and I marked them for this great destiny. I created every part of them, and am their divine Mother. They take their spiritual food from me and find eternal life:

> I come into my garden,
>   my sister, my promised bride.
> I gather my myrrh and balsam,
>   I eat my honey and my honeycomb,
>   I drink my wine and my milk.
> Eat, friends, and drink:
>   drink deep, my dearest friends.
>
> *Song of Songs 5:1, JB*

I am happy with them, not ashamed: they are as I intended them.

Who then can rise up against my handiwork,
or who is there that is not subject to it?
I willed and fashioned mind and heart,
and they are mine;
By my own Right Hand,
I established my chosen ones.
And my Righteous One
goes before them (to light the Way);
And they shall not be separated from my Name,
for it is with them.

(THE ODIST:)

So pray and dwell increasingly in the love of the Lord –
and you who are loved, in the Beloved,
and those who are kept, in him who lives,
and those who are saved, in him who saves –
And you shall become immortal forever,
because of the Name of your Father.

Hallelujah.

No one can hinder the fulfilment of my design. I gave them mind and heart and soul, and they are my dear children. By my divine Power, I made them so. My holy Saviour is with them, all along the Way. Never will they lack my hidden, mystic Name: it will always be with them.

(THE ODIST:)

So meditate and stay close to the loving atmosphere of the Divine. Remain near to the inner Helper. He loves you, and you love him. He protects you, and will bring you to salvation. And you will find eternity, and dwell in it forever:

> Who is able to explain the bond of the love of God?
> Who is sufficient to tell the greatness of its beauty?
> The height to which love lifts us cannot be expressed.
> Love unites us to God.
>
> *1 Clement XLIX:2–5; cf. AF1 p.93*

Ode 9

An ode of rousing spiritual encouragement in which the poet speaks with the voice of the Saviour. You are destined for immortality, he says, through the power of the Word. Success is preordained. So give it all you have got, and carry off the victor's crown!

(THE SAVIOUR:)

Open your ears,
and I will speak to you.
Give me your self,
that I may give you my self –
The Word of the Lord and His will,
the holy Thought that He has thought
concerning His Messiah.

For in the will of the Lord is your life,
and His Thought is everlasting life,
and your end is immortality.
Be enriched in God the Father,
and receive the Thought of the Most High.
Be strong and be redeemed by His grace.

For I bring peace to you, His holy ones,
that those who hear may not fall in war,
that those that have known it (His Thought) may not perish,
that those who have received it may not be put to shame.

Truth is an eternal crown:
blessed are they who set it on their heads.
It is a pearl of great price:
there have been wars on account of this crown.
But the Righteous One has taken it,
and has given it to you.

The Crown of Victory

(THE SAVIOUR:)

Listen with your heart and you will understand what I am saying to you. Listen with your soul, and you will hear the music of my Word. Give your self to me, that I may give my self to you:

> At the cost of all you have,
>   acquire Understanding (Wisdom).
> *Proverbs 4:7, NJB*

For my true self is the Creative Word, the divine will manifested, his Thought, the inner essence of all Saviours. God's will is in your soul, his Thought is eternity, your destination immortality. Accept, then, the treasure of the Lord: let his Thought dwell in your soul. Be powerful in spirit; overcome all obstacles; and let his blessing carry you to salvation.

I bring peace to you, his spiritual children, that not one of you may fail or fall. This spiritual war is one where every one of you will be victorious. None will be left here in the realm of death; no one who has received God's blessed gift will know defeat.

The victor's laurels are assured for all who tread the Path of Truth. Blessedness will be theirs at the ending of the day. This living crown is a priceless gem: men fight about the way to find it. Yet, to you, it has been given by the Saviour:

> Hold her (Wisdom) close, and she will make you great;
>   embrace her, and she will be your pride;
> She will set a crown of grace on your head,
>   present you with a glorious diadem.
> *Proverbs 4:8–9, JB*

Put on, then, the crown of the true Covenant of the Lord,
and all those who have been victorious,
will be written in His Book.
For their Book is the victory that is yours,
and she (victory) knows who you are,
and wills that you should be saved.

Hallelujah.

She (Wisdom) will give him
   the Bread of Understanding to eat,
   and the Water of Wisdom to drink.
He will lean on her and will not fall,
   he will rely on her and not be put to shame....
He will find happiness and a crown of joy,
   he will inherit an everlasting name.

Wisdom of Jesus Ben Sirach 15:3–4, 6, NJB

Well is it for him who wears this crown of the divine Father!

Thousand and Twelve Questions 1:98; cf. TTQ p.136

So place upon your head the true Bond of God; accept his promise of salvation to mankind. And, with all other spiritual champions, see your name entered in the Book of Life. For the Book of Victors is the Word that he has written and has given to you. Victory knows you and desires that you should overcome.

Ode 10

A neatly constructed ode in which the Saviour first presents his credentials – his authority is that of God, through the Creative Word. With this Power, he could bring salvation to the whole world, should he so wish. But he has only come for the motley collection of souls, spread throughout the world, who sincerely seek him.

(THE SAVIOUR:)

The Lord has directed my mouth by His Word:
he has opened my heart by His Light.
He has caused His immortal Life to dwell in me,
and permitted me to speak of the fruit of His peace –
to restore the souls of those who desire to come to Him,
and to lead a goodly band of captives into freedom.

I was strengthened and made powerful,
and the whole world was under my command.
And it became mine for the glory of the Most High,
and of God the Father.
And the people (lit. 'nations') who were scattered abroad
were gathered together.
And I was not made impure by my love for them,
because they worshipped me in high places.
And footprints of light were impressed upon their hearts,
and they walked in the Way of my Life and were saved,
and they became my people for ever and ever.

Hallelujah.

By His Word

All that flows from me is guided by God, through his creative Power. He has filled me with his radiance and beauty. Eternal life has become mine, and I have been appointed to speak of him, and to teach his Way. He has given me the power to heal those souls who truly yearn for him, to take them from the dark dungeon of the world into the light of liberty.

Such strength did I receive that the whole world lay within my power. He appointed me the Saviour of all those who sought his glory.

And those who were destined for me, though they were of every nation and were spread throughout the world, were gathered into one fold. And their darkness did not reduce my light, nor their sins defile me, because they were lifted high into the pure and heavenly realms to worship me:

> For you descended into a great ignorance,
>   but you have not been defiled by anything in it.
> For you descended into a great mindlessness,
>   and your recollection remained.

First Apocalypse of James 28, NHS11 pp.76–77

They trod the stairway to the Light, and became my chosen ones for all eternity.

Ode 11

A lovely ode in which the odist maintains a flow of colourful imagery centred around the 'plant' of his soul. He is pruned by the Holy Spirit, and watered by the Living Water. As a result, he abandons the folly of earthly existence, receives the sun and the dew of divine grace, and is taken into paradise, the garden of delight where 'trees' and 'flowers' bloom and fruit eternally. After that, everything reminds him of God!

By using a word that means both 'to prune' and 'to circumcise', the odist is also indicating the spiritual meaning of the Jewish custom of circumcision.

My heart was pruned (circumcised) and its flower appeared,
and grace sprang up in it,
and it brought forth fruit for the Lord.
For the Most High circumcised me with His Holy Spirit,
and laid bare my inner being towards Him,
and filled me with His love.
And His circumcision became my salvation,
and I ran along the Way, in His peace,
on the Path of Truth.
From the beginning, even to the end,
I received His Knowledge.
And I was established on the rock of Truth,
where He had set me up.

And Speaking Waters touched my lips
from the Lord's Spring, plenteously.
And I drank and was intoxicated
with the Living Water that does not die.
But my intoxication caused no heedlessness:
Rather, I abandoned selfhood,
and turned towards the Most High, my God,
and was enriched by His gift.

Like the Land that Blossoms

The Lord removed from me all that was dead and worthless, and my soul blossomed. By his blessedness, it came to life and flourished, and bore the sweet fruit of divinity. His pruning knife is the deathless Word, by which he reached into my innermost heart, removing my imperfections, filling me with his love. And his pruning brought me to immortal life, for I travelled rapidly on the Road of Truth, and found the peace of God:

> Draw me in your footsteps, let us run.
> Take me, O King, into your chambers.
> *Song of Songs 1:4; cf. JB, NJPS*

From start to finish, in every aspect of his Being, I experienced and knew him. And he placed me securely on his holy Mountain, the Height of all eternity.

And the Music of the Living Waters flowed unhindered in my soul from the Fountain of the Lord. And I quenched my thirst and was filled with an ecstatic joy from the Spring of Life that never dries:

> Whoever drinks of the Water
>   that I shall give him shall never thirst;
> But the Water that I shall give him shall be in him
>   (as) a well of water springing up into everlasting Life.
> *John 4:13–14; cf. KJV*

But this ecstasy of mine caused no loss of intelligence or understanding. Indeed, I was enabled to abandon self (the cause of ignorance) and face the Lord, and to receive the untold wealth of his vast treasury of the Word.

And I forsook the folly that is cast upon the earth:
I stripped it off and cast it from me.
And the Lord renewed me with His garment,
and possessed me with His Light.
And from above He gave me immortal rest,
and I became like the land that blossoms,
and rejoices in its fruits.

For the Lord is like the sun,
shining upon the face of the land:
My eyes were enlightened,
and my face received the Dew,
and my breath (spirit) took pleasure
in the pleasant Fragrance of the Lord.
And He brought me to His paradise,
wherein is the abundance of the Lord's pleasure.

And I contemplated blooming and fruit-bearing Trees,
whose crowns had grown of themselves.
Their branches were in new leaf,
and their fruits were shining,
and from an immortal land arose their roots.
And a River of Gladness watered them,
and all about them,
in the land of eternal life.

Then I worshipped the Lord because of His glory,
and I said, "Blessed, O Lord,
are they who are planted in Thy land,
and who have a place in Thy paradise,
and who thrive in the growth of Thy Trees,
and have passed from darkness into light."

And I abandoned the madness of this world: I rose up in my soul, leaving my body senseless. And God clothed me in his raiment, and dressed me in his glory. From his holy Height, he filled me with a peace past comprehension, and I became like sullen earth, which – at the touch of spring – breaks into flower, sets fruit and comes to harvest.

For the Lord is like the spring sun after winter's dark, shining on the earth, spreading life and light. My spiritual eyes were opened; my soul faced him and received the soft, sweet rain of holiness; and the life within me breathed the Fragrance of his Spirit, and was enraptured and renewed.

He led me to his garden, where he walks and rests in peace. And there, within myself, I saw the great Trees, divisions of the Word, on which his creation grows:

> There are Five Trees for you in paradise
>   which remain undisturbed summer and winter,
>   and whose leaves do not fall.
> Whoever comes to know them
>   will not experience death.
>
> *Gospel of Thomas 19; cf. NHS20 pp.60–61*

The branches of creation that grow upon these Trees are eternally alive, their leaves and fruits pulsating with the joy of being. And the roots of these Trees are anchored in a deathless ground. A stream of bliss and joy flows to their roots and courses through all their sap, flooding everywhere in that eternal realm.

And so my soul was steeped in the natural and ecstatic worship of his bright radiance, and I exclaimed, "How fortunate are they who meet the divine Gardener and are planted in this place; who are given a home in your garden; who grow beneath the shade of your divine Trees; and have emerged from dark and brooding earth into the brightness of the sun."

Behold all thy labourers are fair,
who work good works (or 'practise spiritual practice'),
and turn away from wickedness
to the kindness that is Thine.
For they turned themselves away
from the bitterness of the (evil) trees,
when they were planted in Thy land.

And everything became like a remembrance of Thyself,
and an eternal reminder of thy faithful Servants.
For there is abundant room in Thy paradise, O Lord;
There is nothing therein that is unfruitful,
but everything is filled with Thy fruit.
Glory be to Thee, O God,
the delight of paradise forever.

Hallelujah.

For look, all those disciples who walk resolutely in your Way, bear witness to your beauty. They turn away from the bitter tree of death when they receive your mystic planting:

> I (the Lord) went forth to plant a garden
>> beyond the confines of this world.
> I chose, and planted in it,
>> the plants that grew in the Living Ones.
>
> I will give orders to the Gardener:
> "Attend to my trees, my new plants;
>> attend to my new plants
>> that they sleep not nor slumber;
> That they sleep not nor slumber,
>> that they forget not the Order (*or* Law)
>> that has been given them."

Psalms of Thomas XIII, Manichaean Psalm Book;
cf. MPB p.218, SCMP p.120

Then everything reminds them of you. They see you everywhere, and everything awakens in them memories of the Faithful Ones who serve you – your beloved Saviours. For there is no lack of space in your boundless, fragrant garden:

> In my Father's house are many mansions:
>> if it were not so, I would have told you.
> I go to prepare a place for you.

John 14:2, KJV

There, nothing is barren. Every plant and tree bears your immortal fruit, for this is the land of your eternal harvest.

Glorious are you, O Lord: may we dwell forever in your garden of eternal bliss.

Ode 12

A powerful ode concerning the Word of God as His creative Power, echoing passages from both John's gospel and the *Wisdom of Solomon*. The odist says that God has filled him with experience of His Word, the essence of Truth and Reality. In the same way, the Word fills all creation, is active in all things, penetrates all places. This is the integrating, omnipresent Power by which everything works together as one harmonious whole. Yet, it also makes its dwelling in a human being, a Saviour. Blessed are those, concludes the odist, who come to understand all things through him.

He has filled me with the Word of Truth,
that I may speak the same.
And like flowing waters, Truth flows from my mouth,
and my lips make known His fruits.
And it has caused His Knowledge to abound in me,
because the Mouth of the Lord is the True Word,
and the Door of His Light.

And the Most High has given it (the Word)
to His aeons (inner realms and powers),[3]
which are the interpreters of His beauty,
and the narrators of His Glory,
and the confessors of His Counsel,
and the heralds of His Thought,
and the holy manifesters of His works.

The Word of Truth

The Lord spoke his mystic Word into my inner ear and filled me with the divine Music of his Voice. Now, whatever comes from me reflects his Truth. Truth flows from my heart and lips in all I say or do:

> How shall I understand,
> > except by (the Spirit) which you have shaped for me?
> What can I say unless you open my mouth,
> > and how can I answer unless you enlighten me?
>
> *Thanksgiving Hymns XVIII:5–10 (19); cf. CDSS p.285*

He has given me such experience that the secrets of creation and of his splendour have been revealed to me. I have received the highest blessing from his Mouth:

> All the kings of the earth shall praise you, O Lord,
> > when they hear the words of your Mouth.
>
> *Psalms 138:4; cf. KJV*

For what he utters is his Word of Power that opens the doorway to the realms of Light:

> I am the Door:
> By me, if any man enter in, he shall be saved,
> > and shall go in and out, and find pasture....
> I am the Light of the world:
> He that follows me shall not walk in darkness,
> > but shall have the Light of Life.[4]
>
> *John 10:9, 8:12; cf. KJV*

God has given his creative and sustaining Power to all the worlds and powers of his creation. They shine with his radiance; they tell of his loveliness; they express his desire; they are the messengers of his intent: they bring into being the hidden mysteries of his Mind.

For the subtlety of the Word cannot be told,
and like (the wonder of) its utterance,
so too is its swiftness and its penetration.
For its course is without end:
it never falls, but stands impregnable,
and no man knows its length or breadth.
For like (the incomprehensibility of) its activity,
so too is its end:
For it is the light and the dawning of human thought.

By it, the aeons spoke to one another,
and those that were silent acquired speech.
From it came love and communion,
and they spoke to one another
of that which was within them.
And they were empowered by the Word,
and they knew Him who made them,
because they were in harmony.

The secret ways of his Word cannot be expressed. As wondrous as its outpouring are its speed and reach: it streams on eternally, filling every place. Never failing, unassailable, no man can know its scope – for it is the essential power underlying human life and thought:

> Within her, she is a spirit intelligent, holy,
>   unique, manifold, subtle,
>   active, incisive, unsullied,
>   lucid, invulnerable, benevolent, shrewd,
>   irresistible, beneficent, loving to man,
>   steadfast, dependable, unperturbed,
>   almighty, all-surveying,
>   penetrating all, intelligent,
>   pure and most subtle spirits;
> For Wisdom is quicker to move than any motion;
> She is so pure she pervades and permeates all things.
>
> *Wisdom of Solomon 7:22–24, NJB*

Through it, all creation joins into a single harmony. All regions sing a single symphony. In it is love and union – integration – all differing natures linking hands as one. Knowing the one great Force that drives them all, they work as one vast wholeness of divinity:

> The heavens declare the glory of God,
>   the vault of heaven proclaims his handiwork;
> Day discourses of it to day,
>   night to night hands on the knowledge.
> No utterance at all, no speech,
>   no sound that anyone can hear;
> Yet their voice goes out through all the earth,
>   and their message to the ends of the world.
>
> *Psalms 19:1–4, JB*

For the Mouth of the Most High spoke to them,
and His expression came about by means of it (the Word).
For the habitation of the Word is a Son of Man,
and its truth is love.
Blessed are they who by means of him
have understood everything,
and have known the Lord in His Truth.

Hallelujah.

For everything has flowed out from him. He has spoken: at his command, all things have danced into existence:

> By the Word of Yahweh the heavens were made,
>   their whole array by the Breath of his Mouth....
> He spoke, and it was created;
>   he commanded, and there it stood.
>
> *Psalms 33:6, 9, JB*

Yet, this great Word dwells humbly in a man – a Son of God:

> And the Word was made flesh,
>   and dwelt among us, ...
>   full of grace and Truth.
>
> *John 1:14, KJV*

And his reality is love:

> God is love;
> And he that dwells in love,
>   dwells in God, and God in him.
>
> *1 John 4:16; cf. KJV*

> As the Father has loved me,
>   so have I loved you.
>
> *John 15:9; cf. KJV*

Fortunate are those who have met him and, by his blessings, know the Truth of God.

Ode 13

A delicate little ode that exhorts us to look within and to see in God, as in a mirror, the reality of our own true selves.

Behold, the Lord is our mirror:
open your eyes and see yourselves in Him.
And learn the true nature of your face,
and utter praises to His Spirit.
And wipe away the dirt from your face,
and love His holiness,
and clothe yourself therewith.
Then you will be spotless,
resting at all times with Him.

Hallelujah.

The Lord is our Mirror

Our souls are reflections of the Light of God; we are rays of light from his bright sun:

> A lamp am I to you who look upon Me.
> A mirror am I to you who see Me.
>
> *Acts of John 95; cf. ANT p.253*

> Shine forth, give out light, pure Mirror!
> For in all the worlds you will be called 'Illuminator'.
>
> *Mandaean Prayer Book 323; cf. CPM p.228*

> Take not this mirror away from us!
> Do not obscure our vision (of that) in which we shine.
>
> *Mandaean Prayer, Alma Rishaia Zuta III, PNC p.69*

Open the eyes of the soul and see your self in his self:

> On a sudden, as I faced it,
>   the garment seemed to me like a mirror of myself.
> I saw in it my whole self,
>   moreover I faced my whole self in facing it.
> For we were two in distinction,
>   and one in one likeness.
>
> *Robe of Glory 77–78, Acts of Thomas 112, in PSW p.192*

Then you will know who you really are – and your heart will brim over with tenderness and gratitude to him.

So clear away the coverings of illusion that surround you, obscuring your real inner nature. Put on the garment of his loveliness. Then you will always be with him in purity, eternally.

Ode 14

A humble and loving prayer of the devotee before God. Like a child, his attention is continually directed to his divine Parent. He begs for the support and guidance of God's creative Power; he wishes to be saved from the devil. He requests that he may hear the divine Music of the heavenly realms. But he ends by acknowledging that everything is according to God's mercy, and that only He can truly help.

As the eyes of a son upon his father,
so are my eyes at all times towards Thee, O Lord;
For with Thee is my comfort (lit. 'my breasts')
and my pleasure.
Turn not Thy compassion away from me, O Lord,
and take not Thy kindness from me.
Stretch out to me at all times Thy Right Hand,
and be my guide even unto the end,
according to Thy good pleasure.
Let me be well pleasing before Thee,
because of Thy Glory;
And because of Thy Name,
let me be saved from the Evil One.

As the Eyes of a Son

Like the love of a child for his parents, so is my love for you, O Lord:

> Like the eyes of slaves
>   fixed on their master's hand;
> Like the eyes of a slave girl
>   fixed on the hand of her mistress:
> So our eyes are fixed on Yahweh our God.
>
> *Psalms 123:2, JB*

All sense of security and peace arise from you. Never withhold your grace from me, O God, nor hold back your affection. Lead me always in your Word, according to your will:

> In a moment, my God, your mercy became one with me.
> Because of your strong protection,
>   lo, my diseases (imperfections) passed far from me.
> Lo, joy has overtaken me
>   through your Right Hand that came to me.
>
> *Manichaean Psalm Book; cf. MPB p.153*

May I always please you, Father, and dwell forever in the mystic splendour of your Name, and thus be saved from the Evil One:

> And lead us not into temptation,
>   but deliver us from the Evil One.
>
> *Matthew 6:13, NIV*

And let Thy gentleness, O Lord, abide with me,
and the fruits of Thy love.
Teach me the psalms of Thy Truth,
that I may bring forth fruit in Thee.
And open to me the harp of Thy Holy Spirit,
that with all its melodies I may praise Thee, O Lord.
And according to the multitude of Thy mercies,
so mayest Thou give to me.
But make haste, (O Lord), to grant our petitions,
for Thou alone canst provide for all our needs.

Hallelujah.

May the soft smile of your love surround me, Lord. Teach me to sing the mystic Song of Sweetness; deign to let me hear the hidden Music of your divine Harp playing in glorious symphony through all the heavenly worlds:

> You made of the Word a harp for yourself,
>   playing unceasingly.
> What portrait painter can paint your unadorned face?
> Or what eagle can ascend as you ascend? ...
> What light can I find to compare with your ray?
> *Manichaean Psalm Book; cf. MPB p.118*

Since you are merciful, dear Lord, so show your mercy. Since you are the fountain of generosity, so let your divine gifts flow. But hurry, Lord, for only you can satisfy our hearts.

Ode 15

The odist likens the Lord to the sun, rising like expectant dawn to dispel his spiritual darkness. He speaks of seeing the inner light and hearing the inner sound. He has understood the Word of true Knowledge and relinquished whatever is illusory. Through the generosity of the Lord, he has overcome death, and attained immortality. This, he says, is the treasure given to all those who truly follow Him.

"Sheol" or hell is the abode of the dead. In the present context, it refers to this world.

As the sun is the joy of them that wait for daybreak,
so my joy is the Lord.
For He is my sun,
and His rays have roused me.
His light has dispelled
all darkness from my face:
Through Him I have obtained eyes,
and have seen His holy day.

Ears have become mine,
and I have heard His Truth.
I have received the Thought of Knowledge,
and, through it, I have lived fully.
The way of Error I have discarded,
and I have walked towards Him,
and I have received salvation from Him, ungrudgingly.

He is my Sun

Like the sun for those who await the dawn, so is my Lord to me. He is my light and my sweet happiness. When his divine rays fell upon me, I awoke from the sleep of darkness in this world, and rose from the dead. He has opened the eyes of my soul to see the brightness of his glorious day.

He has restored ears to my deaf soul to hear the Music of his Word. He has revealed his Mind to me, and I have found the Source of Life in him:

> These things I know
>   by the Wisdom which comes from you:
> For you have unstopped my ears
>   to marvellous mysteries.
>
> *Thanksgiving Hymns IX:20–25 (6); cf. CDSS p.254*

Through his True Word, I have stepped off the downward path leading to illusion, and have trod the higher road to him, discovering my salvation.

And according to His generosity,
has He given to me;
And according to His excellent beauty,
has He made me.
Through His Name,
I have been clothed in immortality.
And by His grace,
I have stripped off mortality.
Death has been destroyed before my face,
and Sheol has been overcome by His Word.

Eternal life has arisen
in the land of the Lord;
It has been made known
to His faithful ones;
It has been given unstintingly
to all those that trust in Him.

Hallelujah.

He has been generosity personified. He has re-formed me in the likeness of his loveliness. Through the sweetness of his Name, I have reached eternal life and, by his favour, relinquished mortality and death.

For as my Saviour told me, by his Word he has conquered death. Now eternity beckons me from the home of God. It has been revealed to those who follow him, and generously bestowed upon those who trust their hearts to him.

Ode 16

An ode in praise of the Creative Word. The odist begins by disclosing the source of his own personal inspiration to be the Word, and he goes on to describe the Word as the primal Power in creation.

As the work of the ploughman
is the ploughshare,
And the work of the helmsman
is the piloting of the ship;
So, too, is my work the psalm of the Lord.
The singing of His praises are my art and my service,
because His love has nourished my heart,
and its fruits have poured forth from my lips.

My love is the Lord,
and therefore I will sing to Him.
For I am strengthened by His praise,
and I have faith in Him.
I will open my mouth,
and His Spirit will speak through me
of the glory of the Lord and His beauty –
And the work of His hands,
and the craft of His fingers,
and the multitude of His mercies,
and the power of His Word.

My Work is the Psalm of the Lord

As the ploughman ploughs the land, and the pilot guides the ship, so do I write psalms to the Lord. This is my daily occupation, my art and my service to him. For he has fed me with his love, and the effect of it is on my lips.

The Lord is he who commands my love, and I sing of him alone. Worshipping him fills me with the strength of his Spirit, and I live in him. When I speak, it is his Spirit that is heard, glorying in his majesty and beauty, retelling the ancient tale of all he does – his perfect ordering of all things, the generosity of his mercy, and the supreme power of his Creative Word.

The Word of the Lord discloses the invisible,
and manifests His Thought.
Then the eye sees His works,
and the ear hears His Thought.

It is this (the Word) that has made the broad earth,
and settled the waters in the sea.
By it, He has laid out the heavens and fixed the stars,
and set in order the creation and established it.
Then He rested from His works.
But created things go on as they have been ordained:
they work their works,
and know not how to stand still or to be idle.

And the heavenly hosts are subject to His Word.
The treasury of light is the sun,
and the treasury of darkness is the night.
He made the sun for the day, that it may be light,
while night brings darkness upon the face of the earth.
And the alternation of one to the other,
bears witness to the loveliness of God.

For there is nothing that is outside the Lord:
He was before anything came into being.
And the aeons (the realms of creation)
were made by His Word,
and by the Thought of His heart.
Glory and honour to His Name.

Hallelujah.

The Word reveals his invisible majesty; it expresses his intelligence. By it, his workmanship is discerned, and the divine Song is heard. By his Word, he ordered all the cosmos; then he rested from his works.

But the creation functions in the way he wills; everything moves constantly, busy in his service. The celestial spheres are obedient to him. Sun and moon, light and dark, tell the story of his perfection:

> When God created his works in the beginning,
>> he assigned them their places as soon as they were made.
> He determined his works for all time,
>> from their origins to their distant future.
> They know neither hunger nor weariness,
>> and they never desert their duties.
> None has ever jostled its neighbour,
>> they will never disobey his Word.
>
> *Wisdom of Jesus Ben Sirach 16:26–28; cf. JB, NJB*

For only he exists. He was there when nothing else was. He spoke, and all the realms came into being as the expression of his Mind:

> In the beginning was the Word,
>> and the Word was with God,
>> and the Word was God.
> The same was in the beginning with God.
> All things were made by it,
>> and without it was not any thing made
>> that was made.
>
> *John 1:1–3; cf. KJV, TYN*

So praise and worship him.

Ode 17

The odist, assuming the voice of the Saviour, opens by describing the process of his own salvation as if he had previously been in spiritual darkness. His bondage to the world, he says, has now been severed, and through the "Thought of Truth" – the Creative Word – he has been given the "crown" or garland of eternal life. God has raised his soul to the spiritual Heights, shown him the Way of salvation, and given him the power to break the bonds that bind souls to this world. The odist himself then concludes with an expression of his personal thanks.

(THE SAVIOUR:)

I was crowned by my God,
and my crown is living.
I was absolved by my Lord,
and my salvation is everlasting.
I have been set free from self,
and I am not a man condemned.
My bonds were severed by His hands;
I received the face and likeness of a new person,
and I walked in Him and was saved.

And the Thought of Truth led me on,
and I followed it and went not astray.
And all who saw me were amazed,
and I seemed to them like a stranger.

My Bonds were Severed by His Hands

(THE SAVIOUR:)

My Lord placed a garland of Life upon my head. He made himself my champion, and gave me the deliverance of immortality. He freed me from the lower self that holds the soul in thrall to death. He cut the chains that bound me to this world, renewing all my spirit. And I flew up into the heavenly realms, only resting when I reached eternity:

> I have been saved from Chaos (this world),
>> and released from the bonds of darkness.
> I have come to you, O Light.
>> *Pistis Sophia 149:68; cf. PS pp.298–99*

The true Word became a Path for me from which my feet could never stray:

> Blessed are you, Road of the Teachers,
>> Path of the Perfect,
>> Track that rises up to the Place of Light.
>>> *Mandaean Prayer Book 71; cf. CPM p.58*

> Blessed and praised be this mighty Power, ...
>> house and covering for all souls,
>> Road and Path for all lights and redeemed souls.
>>> *Manichaean Hymns, MBB p.18ff., ML p.64*

> We bless you who have made us
>> meet for the Path of Life.
> We thank you:
>> you are the Creative Word.
>>> *Death of St John; cf. MAA p.57*

And those who knew me were surprised for I had become so
different. And He who knew me and raised me up
is the Most High in all His perfection.
And He glorified me by His kindness,
and raised my understanding to the Height of Truth.

And from thence He gave me the Way of His footsteps,
and I opened the doors that were closed.
And I shattered the bars of iron (that bound me):
for my fetters had grown hot
and had melted before me.
And nothing appeared closed to me,
because I was the Door of everything.

But it was he, the Perfect One, who took me up. By his sweet will, he restored the radiance to my soul, raising my consciousness to the supreme Reality. He made me follow the path that he had trodden, and all barriers to my ascent dissolved. The yearning of my heart set a fire of love ablaze that melted all the chains that held me in bodily captivity:

> Thank Yahweh for his love,
>   for his marvels on behalf of men:
> Breaking bronze gates open,
>   he smashes iron bars.
>
> *Psalms 107:15–16, JB*

I became the Door for those that seek, for the Way to God was cleared and free.

Ode 17

And I went to all my bound ones to set them free,
that I might not leave any man bound or in bondage.
And in my love, I gave them unstintingly,
of my Knowledge and my comfort.
And I sowed my fruits in their hearts,
and transformed them into myself.
And they received my blessing,
and lived;
And they were gathered to me,
and were saved;
Because they were to me as my own members,
and I was their Head.

(THE ODIST:)

Glory to thee, our Head, O Lord Messiah.

Hallelujah.

I sought out all those who were meant for me, and I freed them from their bondage to the body and the world, giving them my love and mystic understanding:

> Some were living in gloom and darkness,
>   fettered in misery and irons....
> Then they called to Yahweh in their trouble,
>   and he rescued them from their sufferings;
> Releasing them from gloom and darkness,
>   shattering their chains.
>
> *Psalms 107:10, 13–14, JB*

I sowed the Seed of Truth in them, and it matured into salvation's fruit, making them like myself. My grace fell upon them, and they found eternal life. They gathered round me and were taken to their Home. For they are to me as the limbs of my body, of which I am the Head.

(THE ODIST:)

Our thanks rise up to you, dear Master, our anointed and appointed one.

Ode 18

An ode that praises the virtue of contact with the inner Creative Word. Likening his soul to his body and its "members", the odist says that the Word has healed all his spiritual imperfections. The Saviour then prays for the salvation of souls from the darkness of the world, after which the odist returns to contrast the reality and truth of God with the illusion and deception of the world. The spiritually ignorant are deceived, he says, but not so the wise who meditate on and are sustained by God's creative Power.

(THE ODIST:)

My heart was raised up and was enriched
by the love of the Most High,
that I might worship Him through His Name.
My members were made strong,
that they might not lose contact with His Power.
Sickness departed from me (lit. 'my body'),
and I (lit. 'it') stood upright in the Lord by His will,
because His kingdom is true and lasting.

(THE SAVIOUR:)

O Lord, for the sake of them who lack (Knowledge of Thee),
do not withhold Thy Word (of Knowledge) from me.
Nor, because of their (imperfect) deeds,
withhold Thy perfection from me.
Let not the Light giver be overcome by darkness,
nor let Truth flee from falsehood.
Thy Right Hand makes salvation attainable (lit. 'victorious').
Let it receive men from all quarters,
preserving all those who are encompassed by evil.

Thy Right Hand makes Salvation Attainable

(THE ODIST:)

My soul ascended and expanded in a love divine, enabling me to glory in his sweet and holy Name – his divine, creative Power. My whole being was revitalized and renewed by communion with the Source of Life. Imperfection left me, and I walked straight on the Path to God, for he is the immortal Power within.

(THE SAVIOUR:)

Dear Father, those in ignorance of you need the assistance of your Word that reaches them through me:

> Do not deprive me of the Word of Truth,
>> since my hope has always lain in your Ordinances (Law).
>>>> *Psalms 119:43, JB*

Overlook their sins, and through me grant them your perfection. Let not the lamplighter lose his flame, nor let Reality abandon the unreal. By your divine, creative Power deliverance can be attained. May its holy doors be open to all souls lost in the dark labyrinth of this world:

> Fight, O sons of Light:
>> yet a little while and you will be victorious.
> He that shirks his burden
>> will forfeit his bride chamber....
> I have become divine again even as I was.
>>> *Manichaean Psalm Book CCXLIX, MPB p.58*

(The Odist:)

Thou art my God:
falsehood and death are not in Thy mouth,
only perfection is Thy will.
Selfhood Thou knowest not,
neither does it know Thee.
Error Thou knowest not,
neither does it know Thee.

And ignorance appeared like dust,
and like the foam of the sea:
And vain people thought that it was something great,
and they came to resemble it and became vain.
But the wise (lit. 'those who knew')
understood and meditated,
and their thoughts remained pure.
For they dwelt in the Mind of the Most High,
and they laughed at those who were walking in Error.
And they spoke the truth,
from the Breath which the Most High breathed into them.

Praise and great honour to His Name.

Hallelujah.

(THE ODIST:)

You are the wellspring of Truth and Life; nothing flows from you but perfect love. Selfhood and egotism are alien to you, and you to them. You are untouched by unreality, for you are the Source of all that truly is.

Ignorance of you is like chaff blown by the wind, like white horses on the waves. Worldly men, lost in the illusion of their separate selves, take it as reality. They are misled by a mirage, entranced by the dream world of their own imagined selves.

But men of spiritual understanding see through the veil by means of contemplation, and their minds are stilled and purified. They are absorbed into the great and saving Power of God, and walk wakeful and carefree among those still lost in dreams. They express only Truth from the Breath of the Spirit that the Divine breathes down upon them:

> The plants (souls) rejoice and flourish
>   in the Perfume of the Saviour
>   which breathes upon them.
>   *Mandaean Prayer Book 83; cf. CPM p.91*

> (Moses) called (it) the Breath of God,[5]
>   because it is the most life-giving thing (in the creation),
>   and God is the Cause (Source) of life.
>   *Philo, On the World's Creation 8; cf. PCW1 pp.22–23, TGH1 p.232*

All worship and glory be to him.

Ode 19

An ode containing imagery that is almost crude, even by modern standards, but is not without parallel in ancient literature. The odist combines two images, the holy "milk" as the Word of God and the birth of a Saviour, born purely from the Wisdom of God, symbolized as the Virgin Mother. He is pointing to the mystic meaning underlying the belief in the virgin birth of Jesus. It is also possible that he is echoing some of the opening verses of John's gospel, since the juxtaposition of thoughts is very similar.

As well as appearing in other early Christian texts, the imagery of "milk" has parallels in *Odes 8* and *35,* while Wisdom as the Virgin also appears in *Ode 33,* calling human beings back to God. Wisdom is a feminine noun in Greek and Semitic languages. Hence, she is portrayed as a pure female – a virgin.

A cup of milk was offered to me,
and I drank it in the sweetness of delight in the Lord.
The Son is the cup (by which I was given the milk),
He from whom the milk came is the Father,
and she who received milk from Him is the Holy Spirit:
Because His breasts were full,
and it was not fitting that
His milk should flow forth to no effect.

The Holy Spirit opened His bosom,
and mingled the milk from the two breasts of the Father,
and gave the mixture to the world without their knowing.
And those who received it (knowingly)
are in the perfection of the Right Hand.

A Cup of Milk was Offered to me

The milk of the Creative Word in the vessel of the Saviour was given to me, and I drank with joy and gladness. The milk of the Word comes from the Father, and is drawn by the Holy Spirit, filling the cup of the Saviour, by whom the milk was given to me. For God overflows with love, desiring only to give his love, and this is his means of sharing it. So the Holy Spirit took the milk of the Word from the bosom of the Father, and brought it into the world. But no one knew of its presence here:

> He (the Word) was in the world,
>   and the world was made by him,
>   and the world knew him not.
> He (the Word) came unto his own,
>   and his own received him not.
>
> *John 1:10–11, KJV*

Only those to whom it was given knew what it was. They are of the family of his Right Hand, of his Word:

> But as many as received him (the Word),
>   to them he gave the power to become sons of God,
>   even to them that believe on his Name.
>
> *John 1:12, KJV*

And the womb of the Virgin (Wisdom)
enfolded it (the milk of God),
and she conceived and gave birth.
And the Virgin became a mother with great compassion.
And she entered labour
and bore a Son without incurring pain,
because it did not happen without divine purpose.

Nor did she require a midwife,
for He had caused her to give life.
She bore, as it seemed, a man by the will of God;
She bore him and made him manifest,
and she received him, according to the great Power.
And she loved him with affection,
and guarded him with kindness,
and made him known with majesty.

Hallelujah.

The holy milk of the Father is dispensed by the pure Virgin of Wisdom, the Creative Word. She is the compassionate Mother who gives birth to the Saviour without pain, for this is the purpose of God, the means by which he distributes his divine milk of love:

> And the Word was made flesh, and dwelt among us
>> and we beheld his glory,
>> the glory as of the Only-Begotten of the Father,
>> full of grace and truth.
>
> *John 1:14, KJV*

Wisdom requires no help, for she is the first expression of the will of God. The Saviour is born from her entirely by his will:

> Which were (was) born, not of blood,
>> nor of the will of man, but of God.
>
> *John 1:13, KJV*

Wisdom is the holy Mother of the Saviour. She cares for him, protects him, and arranges that he becomes known to those whose part it is to know him:

> The nourishment (of the Word) is the milk of the Father, by which alone we babes are fed.... We, believing on God, flee to the Word, "the care-allaying breast" of the Father. And he alone, as is befitting, supplies us children with the milk of love, and only those are truly blessed who suck this breast....
>
> To us infants, who drink the milk of the Word of the heavens, Christ himself is food. Hence, seeking is called sucking; for to those babes that seek the Word, the Father's breasts of love supply milk....
>
> O mystic marvel! The universal Father is one, and one the universal Word; and the Holy Spirit is one and the same everywhere; and one is the only Virgin Mother.... Calling her children to her, she nurses them with holy milk, that is, with the Word.
>
> *Clement of Alexandria, Instructor I:6; cf. WCA1 pp.143–44, 142*

Ode 20

An ode that, like the previous one, seeks to give the inner or mystic meaning behind an external religious belief or practice. The odist describes himself as a "priest of the Lord", going on to say that he considers a true "priest" or holy man to be one who sacrifices himself to the Creative Word ("His Thought"), never injuring others in any way. Such people, he concludes, will be the recipients of divine grace.

I am a priest of the Lord,
and I serve Him as a priest:
To Him I offer the sacrifice of His Thought.
For His Thought is not like the thought of the world,
nor the thought of the flesh;
Nor (is my sacrifice) like that of
them that serve carnally.

The true sacrifice to the Lord is holiness,
and purity of heart and lips.
So present your inner being to Him without shame;
And let not your heart hurt another's heart,
nor your soul hurt another's soul.

True Sacrifice to the Lord is Holiness

I am one who truly ministers to the Lord, serving him in my soul. My offering to him is the surrender of my small self to his eternal Self, of my life to his Life, of the thought of 'me' to his Thought. For his Thought is not like our thought. Our thoughts are of the body and the world. His Thought is a divine and conscious Power.

External sacrifice and worship have no meaning. The real offering to God is purity of mind, spiritual perfection:

> Sacrifice for the Lord is a broken heart.
> A smell of sweet savour to the Lord is a heart
>   that glorifies him that made it.
>
> *Epistle of Barnabas II:10; cf. AF1 p.345*

So come before him with a heart free of imperfection. Never hurt the feelings of another, nor transgress their rights:

> Love your enemies,
>   bless them that curse you,
>   do good to them that hate you;
> And pray for them which despitefully use you,
>   and persecute you....

> All things whatever you wish
>   that men should do to you,
>   do you even so to them.
>
> *Matthew 5:44, 7:12; cf. KJV*

Do not acquire a stranger
with the price of your silver;
Nor seek to deceive your neighbour,
nor deprive him of the covering of his nakedness.

But be clothed in the generous grace of the Lord,
and come into His paradise;
Make yourself a garland from His Tree,
and put it on your head and be glad;
And recline in His rest.

Then His glory will go before you,
and you will receive His kindness and His grace.
And you will flourish (lit. 'become fat') in Truth,
through the worship of His holiness.

Praise and honour be to His Name.
Hallelujah.

Do not purchase a foreigner as a slave, for you know how it feels to be separated from your homeland. Do not indulge in lies, nor reduce others to penury by your greed:

> You must not oppress the stranger;
> You know how a stranger feels,
>   for you lived as strangers in the land of Egypt....
>
> If you take another's cloak as a pledge,
>   you must give it back to him before sunset.
> It is all the covering he has;
>   it is the cloak he wraps his body in;
> What else would he sleep in?
>
> *Exodus 23:9, 22:26–27, JB*

Be worthy of the generosity and munificence of the Lord's grace. Be covered with it, wearing it with honour and humility, and so enter the garden of paradise. Weave a crown of living flowers and branches from the Tree of Life (the Word) that grows there. Seek this joy within your head, and find eternal peace:

> To anyone that overcomes
>   I will give to eat from the Tree of Life,
>   which is in the midst of the paradise of God.
>
> *Book of Revelation 2:7; cf. KJV*

Follow in the footsteps of his splendour, and you will know how generous his love can be. Then you will grow strong in Truth, and understand the nature of Reality. Lose yourself in adoration of his grandeur, listening to the Music of his holy Name.

Ode 21

In a mood of love and gratefulness, the odist pours out his heart to his Saviour for transporting him from the darkness and sickness of this world to the light and wholeness of God. He says that his immortal friend in this ascent has been the Thought of the Lord, the Creative Word, a Helper who has drawn him into joyful communion with the Divine.

I raised my arms to the Height,
on account of the grace of the Lord.
For He has cast my bonds away from me,
and my Helper in his grace has raised me up,
to partake of his salvation.
And I put off darkness
and clothed myself with light.
And my soul acquired members,
free from sickness, suffering or distress.

And supremely helpful to me was the Thought of the Lord,
and his immortal fellowship.
And I was raised up in his light,
and I worshipped before his Face.
And I became near to him,
praising and thanking him.

For he caused my heart to overflow (with his Word),
and it came into my mouth,
and appeared upon my lips.
And the joy of the Lord and His praise lit up my face.

Hallelujah.

On Account of the Grace of the Lord

My heart is full with gratitude to the Most High for the generosity of his blessings. For he has freed me from bondage to my earthly form and from all material things. The helping hand of my beneficent Saviour has raised me from death to the Heights of all eternity:

> Glory be to you, the Defender and Helper
>> of them that come into your refuge!
> You sleep not, and awaken them that are asleep.
> You live, and give life to them that lie in death!
>> *Acts of Thomas 60; cf. ANT p.393*

The darkness within has been transmuted into light, and my soul has become that light, freed from misery, discord and disease:

> You have turned my mourning into dancing:
> You have stripped off my sackcloth (the body),
>> and clothed me with joy.
>> *Psalms 30:11, NJB*

The Word of the Lord, his Thought, is my companion, guide and Helper:

> The divine Teacher is with you always.
> He is a Helper, and he meets you
>> because of the good that is in you.
>> *Teachings of Silvanus 96–97; cf. NHS30 pp.308–11*

This Power has drawn me to the Heights. I ascended on a beam of his celestial glory, and gave my all to him, worshipping inwardly before his shining Face. Now he is my friend and confidante, and I am lost in praise and thankfulness.

His love has filled my heart to overflowing. The joy and ecstasy of the Word pervades my soul and cannot be concealed. His Word finds expression when I speak and act, and his love lights up my face.

Ode 22

The interpretation of this ode is influenced to some extent by whether the Saviour or the soul is understood as the speaker. Here, it has been taken as the soul.

The ode begins by describing the descent of the soul, and the subsequent conquest of all powers in creation, including the devil, as the soul ascends with the help of the creative Power – "Thy Name" or "Thy Right Hand". Probably with a parable of Ezekiel in mind concerning the raising of dry bones, the odist points out that the spiritual meaning of resurrection is for the soul to be given spiritual life, rising up from the grave of the earthly body. He ends by reiterating that everything is founded upon the Rock of the creative Power, and that this is the refuge of those who seek God.

Were the Saviour to be taken as the speaker, the interpretation would be of the Saviour being sent out by God on his mission of mercy to rescue and redeem suffering humanity. Perhaps the odist intended both meanings to be simultaneously understood.

He who caused me to descend from the Height,
also raised me up from the realms below;
He who formed the things that are in the Midst,
also laid them low before me;
He who scattered my enemies and my adversaries;
He who gave me power over bonds
that I might loose them;
He who overthrew by my hands the seven-headed dragon,
and placed me higher than his root,
that I might destroy his seed:
(It is Thee, O Lord).

It is Thee, O Lord

He who sent me out from my eternal home also found and rescued me from exile here below; he who has created all the intermediate heavens also made them stepping stones beneath my feet; he who helped me overcome all human imperfections and surmount the lords of destiny; he who enabled me to break all bodily constraints, setting free my soul to fly to the inner skies; he who helped me overcome the many-faceted negative power, establishing me above his realm and origins, so that I could destroy his progeny – the powers and imperfections that bound me here; you, Lord, are he:

> I have been freed from evil cares
>   and from deeds of corruption;
> And have been delivered from him (the devil)
>   who was alluring me,
>   and inciting me to do those things in which you found me;
> And have understood him (the Saviour)
>   who was saying to me the opposite of them....
>
> And I have destroyed him who through darkness ...
>   made me stumble....
> And I have found the Light, the Lord of the day....
>
> I have been delivered from him whom deception supports,
>   and before whom goes a veil (of ignorance and darkness)....
> And I have found him who shows me fair things
>   that I may experience them,
>   even the Son of the Truth ... who scatters away the mist
>   and enlightens his own creation,
>   and heals the wounds thereof,
>   and overthrows the Enemy thereof.

Acts of Thomas 34; cf. AAA pp.175–76, ANT p.381

> The great dragon was cast out, that old serpent,
>   called the devil and Satan, who deceives the whole world.

Book of Revelation 12:9; cf. KJV

Thou wast there and didst help me:
in every place Thy Name surrounded me.
Thy Right Hand destroyed his (the dragon's) evil poison,
and Thy Hand cleared the Way
for those who believe in Thee.
It (Thy Right Hand) chose them from the graves,
and separated them from the dead.
It took dead bones,
and clothed them with life (lit. 'with flesh').
They were lifeless,
and it gave them energy to live.

Incorruptible was Thy Way and Thy face:
Thou didst bring Thy immortal world
to this world of mortality,
that everything might be dissolved and renewed.

For the foundation of everything is Thy Rock:
upon it Thou hast built Thy kingdom,
and it has become the dwelling place of the holy ones.

Hallelujah.

You were always at my side, helping, guiding and protecting me through the mediation of your mystic Name. For those who follow you, the sword of your Word slays the ancient Enemy, clearing the royal Highway to your kingdom. Your Right Hand plucks them from their bodily tombs, disentangling them from their dead companions. They are as dead; you breathe the Breath of Life into their souls, and watch them spring to life:

> (O) dry bones, hear the Word of Yahweh: ...
> "I am now going to make the Breath (Spirit) enter you,
>   and you will live.
> I shall put sinews on you,
>   I shall make flesh grow on you;
> I shall cover you with skin and give you Breath (Spirit),
>   and you will live;
> And you will learn that I am Yahweh....
>
> "Behold, O my people, I will open your graves,
>   and cause you to come up out of your graves."
> *Ezekiel 37:4–6 (JB), 37:12 (KJV)*

Eternal is your Path and eternal, too, your being. You bring immortality to the region of mortality that the dead may rise.

Everything is built upon your Holy Mountain: you have established your heavenly City there, and it has become the habitation of your blessed children:

> You have set my feet upon rock...
>   that I may walk in the Way of eternity
>   and in the paths which you have chosen.
> *Thanksgiving Hymns XI:1–5 (11); cf. CDSS pp.262–63*

> You have ... established my edifice upon rock;
> Eternal foundations serve for my ground,
>   and all my ramparts are a tried wall
>   which shall not sway.
> *Thanksgiving Hymns XV:5–10 (15); cf. CDSS p.275*

Ode 23

An ode that uses some intriguing imagery to convey the idea of the Word descending from God to this world, and incarnating in the form of a Saviour. The odist begins by speaking of the blessings that come upon those whose part it is to follow the path of the Word. He then depicts the Word as a Letter of Command, bearing the seal of the Supreme. All creation is fascinated by this Letter, he says, but there is none with the authority or power to approach it.

The final destination of the Letter is a Wheel that is wrapped completely by the Letter. The two together then become an irresistible and unstoppable force that mows down all obstructions and negativities. This portrays the fearless and dynamic character of a true Saviour. The "Head" (God or the Word) comes down to the "foot" (man, the physical creation), rolling onward through life with great force, under complete control. In the end, the odist again indicates that the Letter is the Word, when he calls it a "great Volume" that has been "written" by God.

Joy is of the holy ones:
and who shall be clothed in it,
but they alone?
Grace is of the elect,
and who shall receive it,
but they who have trusted in it from the start?
Love is of the chosen ones,
and who shall wear it,
but they who have possessed it from the beginning?
Walk in the Knowledge of the Most High,
and you will know the generosity of the Lord's grace,
His joy, and the fullness of Knowledge of Him.

His Will Descended from on High

Ancient letters were commonly papyrus scrolls, which could be many feet long, sealed with the seal of the sender. The image presented in this ode is of a revolving wheel covered with a long letter-scroll, the size of a "great volume", revolving as it goes – the head or top of the wheel subsequently becoming the foot or base on which the whole is supported.

The highest ecstasy is only known to those blessed souls who receive the gift of grace from the Father's treasury. Blessings fall upon these chosen ones, because they have been destined for it since they left their eternal home. Supreme love is their inheritance, for it has been eternally present with them:

> They who trust in him will understand the Truth,
>> those who are faithful will live with him in love....
> Grace and mercy await the chosen of the Lord,
>> and protection, his holy ones.
>
> *Wisdom of Solomon 3:9, 4:15, JB*

So travel the great Highway to the Lord, and experience his rich munificence. Be steeped in the ocean of his love, and know the depth and wholeness of communion with him.

And his Thought was like a Letter:
His Will descended from on high.
It was sent like an arrow from a bow,
shot forcefully.
And many hands rushed upon the Letter,
to seize it, to take it and to read it.
But it escaped their fingers,
for they were in awe of it,
and of the seal that was upon it;
For they were not permitted to loose its seal,
since the Power invested in it
was greater than they.

His Word is like a Letter, containing his Will or his Command. Sent from the Most High, it is shot like an arrow from a bow, aimed forcefully at its mark:

> The Lord ... poured forth and enlarged the goodness and grace of his divinity by sending his consubstantial Son – the Son of Self-existence. In a befitting way, his Will descended towards men: he sent his Beloved, the Begotten of himself, that is, his very Image.
>
> *Mar Abd Yeshua; cf. NR2 p.39*

Many glimpsed this Letter as it sped, and tried to grasp it, and to read its contents. But it eluded them, for it was not their part to know it. Moreover, they were awed by Whose seal it bore, having no warrant to tamper with it, for it carried the authority of divinity, a power far greater than their own:

> (God) sent a Letter,
>   which he sealed with his Essence (Word),
>   which has no beginning.
>
> *Chaldaean Breviary, BCB I:44, OPS p.338*

> A Letter, communication and purity
>   came to me from the house of Life (eternity).
> Its fastening is Water, its garland is Light,
>   its weapon the Living Word,
>   and its seal the Chosen Pure One (the Saviour).
> Every man who opens it and reads therein shall live.
>
> *Mandaean Prayer Book 63; cf. CPM p.52*

But those who saw the Letter, went after it,
that they might learn where it would alight,
and who would read it,
and who would hear it.
But a Wheel received it and was wrapped by it,
for in it (the Letter) was a sign
of dominion and (divine) government.
And everything that disturbed the progress of the Wheel,
it (the Letter and Wheel combined)
mowed and cut down.
It overwhelmed a multitude of adversaries,
and it clogged up rivers with earth
(and stopped them flowing);
It crossed over them,
and uprooted many forests,
making a broad and open Way.

Everyone who caught sight of the Letter followed it to discover the one to whom it was addressed. A Wheel was the recipient, which was enfolded by the Letter. The Saviour is the Wheel; the Letter is the Word enveloping the Saviour. Nothing can stand in the way of this divine alliance. All human imperfection, all powers of destiny, all burden of past sin – nothing is a hindrance to this revolving Wheel, wrapped entirely by the Letter. The Word and the Saviour, which are one, clear a wide Highway to the Lord.

The Head came down to the feet,
for the Wheel ran on its foot,
along with the Letter that was covering it.
And the Letter was one of command,
for all realms were under its jurisdiction.
And the head that was stamped (on the seal)
was the Head that was revealed,
even the Son of Truth from the Most High Father,
whose inheritance is power over everything.

And the speculations of the many came to nothing,
and all those who led others astray,
hastened and fled away.
And the persecutors were extinguished and blotted out.

For the Letter was a great Volume,
written wholly by the Finger of God.
And the name of the Father was upon it,
and of the Son and of the Holy Spirit,
to reign forever and ever.

Hallelujah.

The Word comes down to the physical universe, the Head manifesting at the foot, like the top of a wheel becomes its base as it revolves: God as the Word, incarnate as the Saviour, comes down to the foot of his creation, the material world.

The Letter is the Command or Will of God, and the whole creation is subject to this Word:

> When he decrees a matter,
>   he says to it "Be!"
> And it is.
>
> *Qur'an 2:117*

The Letter's seal, its stamp of authority, has the head of the Son of God embossed upon it. But the true Son is the primal, "Only-Begotten" emanation of the Father, the Word that governs everything.[6]

In its presence, the speculations and interpretations of priests and philosophers become meaningless. They lose their capacity to confuse others. Enemies in this world or imperfections of the mind are also deprived of their power to create disturbance.

The Letter is the vast Book wherein all creation is written. Nothing is greater than it, and nothing is outside it. It is written entirely by God. The essence of its being is the Father, the Saviour and the Creative Word. These three reign over and sustain creation for as long as it continues. Through them, man can find God:

> Had that Book not been manifested (as a Saviour), none of those who believe in salvation could have attained it.
>
> *Gospel of Truth 20; cf. NHS22 pp.86–87*

Ode 24

An ode describing the impact of the Messiah's presence on the various levels of creation. Becoming aware of him, the inhabitants of the heavenly realms are awed, the dwellers in hell are disturbed, and most of those who live in this world find little consolation either. In their suffering, they call out to God for help. But, "because the Truth was not in them", their miseries are not alleviated, and they stay in the realm of death. Nevertheless, says the odist, the Way of the Word was brought to the world, and those who recognized it, found God.

The ode, which contains a number of obscurities, begins with an allusion to the gospel account of Jesus' baptism.[7] According to Matthew, when Jesus was baptized by John the Baptist, the "heavens were opened unto him", meaning that he was immediately able to travel through the heavenly realms. At the same time, the Holy Spirit is described metaphorically as descending upon him in the form of a dove, and a "voice" is heard from heaven. In the ode, the "Voice" of the dove symbolizes the inner sound or music of the Holy Spirit.

The dove fluttered over the head of our Lord Messiah,
because he was her head.
And she sang over him,
and her Voice was heard.

The Voice of the Dove

The dove of the Holy Spirit is the protector and the essence of our Saviour, for he is the king of the Spirit:

> The living Kingdom shall be revealed again,
>   the love of God, the white dove.
> For the Holy Spirit was likened to a dove.
>> *Manichaean Psalm Book, MPB p.156*

> You are a Spring, O Jesus, ...
> You are a Spring of Living Water,
>   the mysteries of the Father being revealed to you....
> You are the holy dove ...
>   that floats in the skies (the inner realms).
>> *Manichaean Psalm Book; cf. MPB p.185*

The dove sings the Song of Sweetness, making her Voice heard and her presence felt in all regions of creation:

> And I heard a Voice from heaven,
>   as the Voice of many waters,
>   and as the Voice of a great thunder:
> And I heard the Voice of harpers
>   harping with their harps.
>> *Book of Revelation 14:2, KJV*

> This mystery, this explanation,
>   is a Voice that explains voices,
>   a Word that interprets all words.
>> *Thousand and Twelve Questions I:231;*
>> *cf. TTQ p.168*

And the inhabitants were awed,
and the foreigners trembled.
And the birds took to flight,
and all creeping things died in their holes.
And the underworlds were opened and they looked out,
and they cried to the Lord like women in labour.

But no nourishment was given to them,
because he (the Messiah) was not their portion.
And the underworlds were sealed (lit. 'immersed')
with the seal (lit. 'immersion') of the Lord;
And they perished in the thought
in which they had existed from the beginning.
For they had laboured (as in childbirth) from the beginning,
though the ending of their labour
would have been the coming of eternal life.

The souls in the higher realms, aware of the divine presence of the Voice or Word of the Saviour, are in awe of it. They become silent. Nor can other negative forces stand before it. The nether worlds also feel this presence. They call out to the Saviour in their distress, but he is not meant for them. Their role and destiny has been ordained by God from the beginning of creation as places of affliction, and they remain that way, though their inhabitants' only hope of deliverance is contact with a Saviour.

And all those who were imperfect met their end,
because they were unable
to utter the Word in their defence,
so that they might live (lit. 'continue').

And the Lord destroyed the suppositions
of all those who had not the Truth in them.
For they who were proud of heart
were deficient in wisdom;
And they were rejected,
because the Truth was not with them.

For the Lord (Messiah) disclosed his Way,
and spread abroad his grace;
And those who recognized it (his Way),
knew his holiness.

Hallelujah.

In this world, the imperfect continue to be so. They are dead, and so they remain, for the only defence against the law of justice is the Word, and most souls have no access to it. They have replaced the divine Word with human words. But the hollowness of the theories and speculations of philosophers and theologians is exposed by the Saviour. Vanity and selfhood have clouded their wisdom; and though they seek Truth, they do not find it, for they are full of falsehood.

Even so, the Lord has paved a broad Highway to himself, and his blessings flow generously upon those who recognize and tread the Path to him, and come to know his Holy Spirit.

Ode 25

After a number of complex odes, we return with some relief to a beautiful and simple expression of the odist's gratitude for the blessings of liberation and spiritual light that have been given him. With the help of the Word, the forces holding him down have been vanquished. He has met the spiritual form of the Saviour inside; light has appeared within; and he has been enabled to leave his body and discover the wholeness of the Spirit. Through the power of the mystic Name, he has been forgiven, and has come to know the peace of eternity.

I was rescued from my bonds
and unto Thee, my God, I fled;
For Thou art the Right Hand of my deliverance,
and my Helper.
Thou hast restrained them that rise up against me,
and I have seen them no more;
Because Thy face was with me,
which saved me, by Thy grace.
For I was despised and rejected in the eyes of many,
and in their eyes I was as lead (or 'as one who is lost ').
But strength was given me from Thee, and help.

I was Rescued from my Bonds

I was released from earthly bondage and flew to you, dear Lord. The Right Hand of your Word imparted strength to me, guiding me to liberty. Your unlimited Power overcame my limitations and the forces standing in my way, and they vanished like the night. For your beauteous heavenly form was with me, to help and protect me.

I had been held of no account by many, but you came, and gave me strength to rise above the world. You enlightened me; light shone in my soul from every quarter; I was transmuted into light; your Spirit clothed me in radiance, and I rose up from my bodily form:

> The gates of the skies (heavens)
>   have opened before me through the rays of my Saviour,
>   and his glorious Likeness of Light.
> I have left the garment upon the earth,
>   the senility of diseases that was with me.
> The immortal robe I have put upon me.

Manichaean Psalm Book CCLXIV, MPB p.81

Thou didst set a lamp at my right hand and at my left,
that in me there may be nothing that is not bright.
And I was covered with the covering of Thy Spirit,
and I removed from myself my garment of skin.
For Thy Right Hand raised me up,
and caused sickness to pass away from me.
And I became strong in Thy Truth,
and holy in Thy holiness.
And all my adversaries were afraid of me,
and I became the Lord's, through the Name of the Lord.
And I was absolved by His kindness,
and His rest is for ever and ever.

Hallelujah.

O God, give me light in my heart, ... light in my eye, ...
    light in my flesh, light in my bones,
    light before me and light behind me,
    light at my right hand, light at my left hand,
    light above, light beneath me.
O God, augment my light and give me light
    and procure me light.

Abu Talib I:6, Book of the Dove, BD p.lxxxvii

I was filled with Truth, sanctified by your sanctity. The powers of darkness stood aside as I rose up and flew to God, blessed by his Holy Name. By his tender mercy, all my past was washed away:

Surely goodness and mercy shall follow me
    all the days of my life:
And I will dwell in the house of the Lord forever.

Psalms 23:6, KJV

Ode 26

The odist is filled with praise and appreciation for divine blessings, joyously received. As so many times before, he makes it clear that the source of this grace is the Word – here depicted as "His holy Song" and "His Harp". The allusion is to the divine Music of the Word that enraptures his soul. Every part of his being is absorbed in this divine Power; this is how he praises and gives thanks to the Lord. And he feels that there is no place or situation where God is not to be praised and thanked for His perfection. He says that no one can truly praise the Lord in words. It is sufficient to experience the rest of eternal beatitude, as the Saviours – the "Psalmists" – do. They are an ever flowing spring, providing Living Water for those souls who seek it.

I poured out praise to the Lord,
for I am His.
And I will recite His holy Song (lit. 'Ode'),
for my heart is with Him.
His Harp is in my hands,
and the Odes of His Rest shall not be silent.

I will cry unto Him with all my heart,
I will praise and exalt Him with all my members.
For from the East to the West,
praise is His;
And from the South to the North,
thanksgiving is His.
And from the crest of the hills to their furthest part,
perfection is His.

The Odes of His Rest shall not be Silent

I glory in the wonder of God, for I am a part of him. I listen to the blessed Symphony on high, and my soul dances in his presence. The celestial Harp has become mine, playing the mystic Song of heaven in unceasing rapture:

> Then will I play on the Zither of Deliverance
>   and the Harp of Joy,
>   [on the Tabors of Prayer] and the Pipe of Praise
>   without end.
>
> *Thanksgiving Hymns XIX:20–25 (22), CDSS p.289*

I yearn for him with all my soul, I delight in him and worship him with every fibre of my being. High and low is his magnificence; near and far, gratitude for his blessings; throughout all creation, the expression of his perfect transcendence is to be found.

Who can write the Odes of the Lord
or who can read them?
Or who can train his soul for Life,
that his soul may be saved?
Or who can be so founded upon the Most High,
that he may speak with His mouth?
Who is able to interpret the wonders of the Lord?
For he who interprets will pass away,
while that which is interpreted will remain.

It is enough to know and to rest
for the Psalmists remain in rest –
Like a river springing from an abundant source,
flowing to the help of them that seek it.

Hallelujah.

None can write the unwritten Song of God that plays eternally; none can recite all its endless melodies. None can be the author of his own salvation, or by himself, descry eternity. Who can describe the glories of God and the mysteries of creation? Even he who so describes will die, while creation continues on, unheeding:

> Who among all your creatures
>   is able to recount [your wonders]?
>   *Thanksgiving Hymns XIX:20–25 (22); cf. CDSS p.289*

> Who among your great and marvellous creatures
>   can stand in the presence of your glory?
> How then can he (man) who returns to his dust?
> For your glory's sake alone have you made all these things.
>   *Thanksgiving Hymns XVIII:10–15 (19); cf. CDSS p.285*

It is sufficient to seek the Divine and to rest in the bliss of the Lord. For the Master singers dwell in his peace and bliss. They are streams of Living Water from the ocean of God's love, seeking those who thirst.

Ode 27

A neat little ode based upon the Christian symbol of the Cross, and the early Christian cruciform attitude for prayer. But the odist is seeing the mystic meaning of the Cross, commonly described as the Tree, and equated with the Tree of Life – another term for the Creative Word. Dying on the Cross or Tree of Life during prayer meant leaving the body during spiritual practice, and communing with the Word within.

I stretched out my hands,
and blessed my Lord;
For the extension of my hands
is His Sign.
And my expansion
is the upright Tree.

Hallelujah.

The Cross of Life

I opened my heart in praise of God, and my soul thanked him in silent joy. This opening is the Cross of Life on which, in mystic prayer, I daily die. The Word is the Saviour's insignia. And I am spread upon the Tree of Life, by which I live:

The Cross of Light that gives life to the universe,
    I have known it and believed in it:
For it is my dear soul, nourishing every man,
    at which the blind are offended
    because they know it not.

Manichaean Psalm Book CCLXVIII; cf. MPB p.86

Rejoicing, I come to you, O Cross,
    the Life giver, Cross whom I know now to be mine;
I know your mystery,
    for you have been planted in the world
    to make unstable things secure.

Your head stretches up into heaven,
    that you may be as a sign for the heavenly *Logos,*
    the head of all things....

O Cross, instrument of salvation, most skilfully devised,
    given unto men by the Highest; ...
O Cross, Life-giving Tree, roots planted on earth,
    fruit treasured in heaven;
O Cross, most venerable sweet thing and sweet Name;
O Cross, most worshipful,
    who bears as grapes the Master, the True Vine....
You who bring the worthy back to God through *gnosis,*
    and summon sinners home through repentance!

Acts of Andrew; cf. ANT pp.359–60, FFF pp.445–46

Ode 28

The odist first professes his joy and awareness of the protection afforded him by the Holy Spirit, symbolized as a dove. He is like a young bird in the nest or an unborn babe in his mother's womb. His soul is so united to his Saviour that even death cannot separate them, for he is already familiar with the nature of death and has attained immortality.

The Saviour then takes up the theme, describing, in the first person, the life and death of Jesus. He was despised for his love, but persecution did not hinder his ministry. He saw his persecutors like rabid dogs who ignorantly bite their caring masters, and he was unaffected by them; for he had within himself the sweet Water of the Word, which they feared. Although they tried to kill him, they could not, for the eternal Word cannot be destroyed. Even those who followed after were unable to destroy his memory, for the divine Thought or Word precedes everything.

As the wings of doves above their nestlings,
and the mouths of the nestlings towards their mouths,
so also are the wings of the Spirit over my heart.
My heart is gladdened and leaps with joy,
like the babe who leaps for joy in his mother's womb.

I had faith, therefore I was at rest,
for faithful is he in whom I put my faith.
He has richly blessed me,
and my head is with him.
No sword can separate me from him,
nor any blade.
For I have made ready before death comes,
and have been sheltered beneath his immortal wings.

Deathless Life Embraced me

As doves feed and care for their young, so does the Holy Spirit guard and nourish me. My soul is filled with ecstasy, and leaps within, like a baby safe and warm in his mother's womb.

Faith in my Faithful One has given me eternal peace, and he will never let me down. He has conferred a treasury of grace upon me. He dwells within my head, and my soul is filled with him alone. Not even death can part us, for I have learned to die before my time, and have sought sanctuary like a nestling beneath his eternal, deathless wings:

> This which is called death, is not death,
>   but a release from the body.
> For which reason, I gladly receive
>   this release from the body:
> That I may depart and see him
>   that is beautiful and full of mercy,
>   him that I love, him who is my Beloved.

Acts of Thomas 160; cf. AAA pp.291–92, ANT p.434

Deathless Life has embraced me,
and kissed me;
And from that Life is the spirit within me,
and it cannot die, because it is Life itself.

(THE SAVIOUR:)

They who saw me, marvelled at me,
because I was persecuted;
And they supposed that I had been swallowed up:
for I seemed to them as one of the lost.
And my oppression
became my salvation;
And I became an abomination to them,
because there was no anger in me.
And because I always did good to every man,
I was hated.

Immortal Life has enfolded me, and made itself my intimate. From the Spring of Life has my soul arisen, and it can never be extinguished, for it is a drop of the eternal Source.

(THE SAVIOUR:)

Those who saw me were astonished. They saw the enmity of others, and thought my mission to have failed, for outwardly I seemed to be without support. But the Divine was with me and, through that persecution, I gave emancipation, taking on myself the sins of others. And they hated me because I did not strike back, but repaid enmity with love:

> To many, I have seemed an enigma,
>   but you are my firm refuge.
> My mouth is full of your praises,
>   filled with your splendour all day long.
>
> *Psalms 71:7–8, JB*

And they surrounded me like mad dogs,
who ignorantly attack their master;
For their thinking is corrupt,
and their understanding perverted.
But I was carrying (Living) Water in my Right Hand,
(that I might turn away their fire).

And because of my sweetness,
their bitterness did not touch me.
And I did not perish (though they had bitten me),
for I was not their kin,
nor was my birth like theirs.
And though they sought my death,
it was impossible for them to accomplish it;
Because I was older even than their memory,
and in vain did they attack me.

And those who came after me,
sought in vain to erase the memory
of him who was before them;
For nothing is prior to the Thought of the Most High,
and His heart is greater than all human wisdom.

Hallelujah.

They were like rabid dogs, mad with rage, who unwittingly attack the one who feeds them. For their minds were unknowing, and their wisdom clouded. But I had with me, in my Right Hand, the Living Water of the Creative Word, flowing from the eternal Spring of love, which they despised, like hydrophobics who fear water, though they desperately need it. And its sweetness gave me strength to tolerate their hatred. And I did not die, for I was not like them, nor had I come into this world like them, carrying a burden of past sin, weighing down the soul. They tried to kill me, but they did not understand. My Essence is older than their existence, and is beyond the transient vagaries of birth and death:

> Yahweh created me (Wisdom)
>> when his purpose first unfolded,
>> before the oldest of his works.
> From everlasting I was firmly set,
>> from the beginning,
>> before the earth came into being.
>> *Proverbs 8:22–23, JB*

And those who followed after tried to efface all memory of me, but Truth can never die. For I was not my bodily form, and Reality can never be destroyed. Nothing is older than the Mind of God: his Wisdom encircles all creation.

Ode 29

The odist expresses his boundless faith in the Lord and in the Saviour. It is a faith founded upon experience, for he has been raised up from the death of this world to the heights of eternal life, and has known the grace and goodness of God. All his human imperfections have been vanquished. He has met and known the Messiah, who has armed him with the Word by which to gain victory in the spiritual war.

The Lord is my hope,
I shall not be ashamed of Him.
For according to His glory,
so He made me;
And according to His goodness,
so He gave to me;
And according to His mercy,
so He raised me up;
And according to His excellent beauty,
so He established me on high;
And He brought me up out of the depths of Sheol,
and from the mouth of death, He drew me.
And I laid low my enemies,
and He supported me by His grace.

The Lord Overthrew my Enemies

I live in the faith of God; and will not deny him. For he it is who made me; he who gave me life and love; he who raised me up, and took me to the highest heaven.

He found me here, in the realm of death, and drew me out:

> I thank you with all my heart, Lord my God,
>   I glorify your name forever.
> Your love for me has been so great,
>   you have rescued me from the depths of Sheol.
>
> *Psalms 86:12–13, JB*

He is kind and gracious, glorious and beautiful. He overturned all barriers in my way; he helped me to overcome my imperfections; he blessed my faltering efforts:

> Clay and dust that I am,
>   what can I devise unless you wish it,
>   and what contrive unless you desire it?
> What strength shall I have
>   unless you keep me upright?
>
> *Thanksgiving Hymns XVIII:5–10 (19); cf. CDSS p.285*

For I believed in the Lord's Messiah,
and it was clear to me that he was the Lord.
And he showed me his Sign,
and he led me by his Light.
And he gave me the Staff of his Power,
that I might subdue alien thoughts,
and humble the power of the mighty (Evil One):
To make war by his Word,
and to gain victory by his Power.

And the Lord overthrew my enemies by his Word,
and they became like chaff
that is carried away by the wind.
And I gave praise to the Most High,
because He had magnified his servant
and the son of his handmaid.

Hallelujah.

For I have known the Saviour. I recognized that he was God himself, because he revealed to me his insignia of the Word, and led me into the Light. He gave me his support and staff, his Tree of Life, by whose power I overcame the unruly legions of my thoughts, and laid low the mighty Evil One:

> Even though I walk
>> through the valley of the shadow of death,
>> I will fear no evil.
> For you are with me.
>
> *Psalms 23:4; cf. KJV*

I fought a holy battle by his Word and was victorious:

> O my Father, my God, my Saviour, my King:
>> I will be a champion for you,
>> I myself will go out and fight....
> O my Father, my God,
>> the giver of the victory to them that are his,
>> give me these (eternal) garlands,
>> for I also have laboured in the fight.
>
> *Manichaean Psalm Book; cf. MPB pp.148–49*

God has helped me to surmount all human imperfections: they have lost their hold on me, dispersed like leaves in an autumn gale. And I thank the Lord most High, because he has filled me with himself, I – a man of small account:

> I thank you, my God,
>> for you have dealt wondrously to dust,
>> and mightily towards a creature of clay!
> I thank you, I thank you!
>
> *Thanksgiving Hymns XIX:1–5 (21); cf. CDSS p.287*

Ode 30

A stirring invitation to enjoy the ecstasy and peace of the Living Waters of the Word. This is a favourite theme among the ancient writers, with echoes in Isaiah, the Wisdom literature, the gospels, and other places.

Draw for yourselves water
from the Living Spring of the Lord,
because it has been opened to you.
Come, all you who thirst, and take a draught,
and rest beside the Spring of the Lord.
For fair it is and pure,
and gives rest to the soul.

Sweeter by far than honey are its waters,
and the honeycomb of bees cannot be compared with it;
Because it flows forth from the lips of the Lord,
and from the heart of the Lord is its Name.

And it came unhindered and unseen,
but until it sprang up within them,
men knew it not.
Blessed are they who have drunk from it,
and have found rest thereby.

Hallelujah.

Come, all you who Thirst

The fountain of eternity is hidden in your soul. Seek there, and discover the sweet Waters of immortal life.

If you yearn for God within, then come and quench your thirst. Peace and happiness can be found in the quiet meadows of your heart. For this sweet Water is music to the soul, and brings stillness from above:

> O come to the water all you who are thirsty;
>   though you have no money, come!
> Buy corn (*i.e.* bread) without money, and eat,
>   and, at no cost, wine and milk.
> Why spend money on what is not bread,
>   your wages on what fails to satisfy?
> Listen, listen to me,
>   and you will have good things to eat
>   and rich food to enjoy.
> Pay attention, come to me;
>   listen, and your soul will live.
>
> *Isaiah 55:1–3, JB*

If any man thirst, let him come to me; let he who believes in me, drink. As the scripture says, 'Out of his breast (from within himself) shall flow rivers of Living Water.'

John 7:37–38; cf. JB, KJV, RSV

And when the happy soul stretches forth its own inner being as a most holy drinking vessel – who is it that pours forth the sacred measures of true joy but the *Logos,* the Cup-bearer of God and Master of the feast – he who differs not from the

draught he pours – his own self free from all dilution, who is the delight, the sweetness, the forthpouring, the good cheer, the ambrosial drug ... whose medicine gives joy and happiness.

Philo, On Dreams II:37; cf. PCW5 pp.554–55, TGH1 pp.245–46

Come and eat my bread,
  drink the wine I have prepared!
Leave your folly and you will live,
  walk in the ways of Understanding (Wisdom).

Proverbs 9:5–6; cf. JB

Come to me, all you who labour and are heavy laden,
  and I will give you rest.
Take my yoke upon you, and learn from me;
For I am meek and lowly in heart,
  and you will find rest for your souls.
For my yoke is easy, and my burden is light.

Matthew 11:28–30; cf. KJV

No known flavour can be compared to it; nothing is sweeter than its taste, or gives more happiness. For it springs from the mouth of Love, and is known by a secret Name:

Come unto me all you who desire me,
  fill yourselves with my fruits;
For my memory is sweeter than honey,
  my inheritance than honeycomb.

Wisdom of Jesus Ben Sirach 24:19–20; cf. in OPJG p.61

And yet, for most people, its presence is neither seen nor heard. Unless by grace, men find the Way, they will never know of it. Favoured are those who drink from it in the still meadows of their heart.

Ode 31

An ode that describes the coming of the Saviour. At his appearance in the world, spiritual darkness gives way to spiritual light. He imparts a message of hope, gathers his children around himself, and offers them to God. The Saviour then takes up the theme, encouraging the souls of this world to relinquish their suffering, and seek their true spiritual birthright. For despite all the persecution he (as Jesus) had to face, he never forgot his purpose in being here: to bring redemption to those who were destined for him.

The depths melted before the Lord (the Messiah),
and darkness vanished at his appearance.
Error went astray,
and perished before him.
Ignorance was rendered impotent,
and sank beneath the Truth of the Lord.

He opened his mouth and spoke grace and joy:
he sang a new song of praise to His Name.
He lifted up his voice to the Most High,
and offered to Him the sons that were in his hands.
And his petition was accepted,
for his holy Father had already decreed it to be so.

The Depths Melted before the Lord

The world fades to insignificance in the presence of the Saviour, and inner darkness turns to light. Illusion relinquishes its beguiling hold, and spiritual ignorance dissolves, replaced by an awareness of the Truth:

> Lo, I sleep and awake,
>> and I shall no more go to sleep.
>>> *Acts of Thomas 142, ANT p.427*

> Come in peace, Awakener of the sleeping
>> and Arouser of the sleepy!
> You who make the dead arise!
>> *Manichaean Hymns, MM1:312.16, ML p.108*

Gladness and blessings he brings with him – new life to old souls by the practice of the sacred Name. He petitions God for the redemption of his children, and his prayer is heard, for it has already been ordained:

> This is the will of the Father who has sent me,
>> that of all those whom he has given me
>> I should lose none,
>> but should raise them up again at the last day....
> I pray for them: I pray not for the world,
>> but for those whom you have given me;
>> for they are yours....
> Father, I will that they also,
>> whom you have given me, be with me where I am;
> That they may behold my glory, which you have given me:
> For you loved me before the foundation of the world.
>> *John 6:39, 17:9, 17:24; cf. KJV*

(The Saviour:)

Come forth, you who have suffered,
and receive joy.
And by His grace come into the inheritance of your souls,
and take to yourselves immortal life.

And they condemned me when I stood up,
I who had been found not guilty.
And they divided my goods,
although nothing was owing to them.
But I endured and held my peace and was silent,
that I might not be disturbed by them.
And I stood unshaken as an immovable rock
that is pounded by waves and yet endures.
And with humility I bore their bitterness,
that I might redeem my people, and teach them;
And that I might not nullify the promises of the patriarchs,
whose seed I had promised to redeem.

Hallelujah.

(THE SAVIOUR:)

Awake! Stand up! Leave behind the misery of this world and know the gladness of eternity:

> Why do you sleep, my soul,
>   and why do you not bless the Lord?
>
> *Psalms of Solomon III:1, AOT p.658*

Through divine mercy, discover who you really are, and enter the bliss of immortality:

> There was within me a stillness of silence
>   and I heard the Blessedness
>   whereby I knew my real self.
>
> *Allogenes 60; cf. NHS28 pp.222–23*

They condemned me when I came before them, though they knew I had done no wrong. They shared my possessions among them, although I owed them nothing:

> I can count every one of my bones,
>   while they look on and gloat at me.
> They divide my garments among them,
>   and cast lots for my clothes.
>
> *Psalms 22:17–18; cf. KJV, NJB*

But I kept quiet, saying not a word, for they did not disturb my peace. I was like a rock at sea, buffeted by the storms, but never moving.

With love, I responded to their hatred, for I had a purpose to fulfil: to take my children to their home on high, as promised by the prophets and patriarchs of old.

Ode 32

A succinct expression of the spiritual strength and happiness
known to those who have inner contact with the mystic
Word.

The blessed have joy within their hearts,
and light from Him who dwells in them,
and the Word of Truth that is self-existent.
And they receive their strength
from the holy Power of the Most High:
He who rests unchanging for ever and ever.

Hallelujah.

The Blessed have Joy

The blessed experience the bliss of his love, and see his light, and hear his Word within themselves.

Their strength comes from the great, creative Power of the One who abides unshaken and unperturbed through all eternity:

> Blessed are they that receive the Wisdom of Jesus Christ,
>   for they shall be called sons of the Most High.
> Blessed are they that have kept their baptism pure,
>   for they shall rest with the Father and with the Son.
> Blessed are they that have compassed
>   the understanding of Jesus Christ,
>   for they shall be in light.

Acts of Paul II:6, ANT p.273

Ode 33

An ode that depicts the interplay between the negative power (the "Corruptor" or the devil) and the creative Power (the Word or Wisdom of God). This "Corruptor" leads every soul in the world astray, for few recognize the game he is playing, and they unwittingly accept his leadership. Only the grace of the Word can rescue a soul, rendering the "Corruptor" harmless. The term 'Corruptor' is derived from the use of 'corrupt' as a description of the material world, referring to its changing, contaminated and unclean character.

Personifying Wisdom as a Virgin – and by implication indicating the real nature of the holy 'mother' of Jesus – the odist then echoes Proverbs, where Wisdom calls out to human beings to take her help and refuge in relinquishing the transient and seeking the real. Those who follow her will learn the mystic way of Wisdom, the path of the Holy Name.

Since it opens rather abruptly, it is possible that the beginning of the ode is missing.

Grace came swiftly and banished the Corruptor,
descending upon him to render him harmless;
For he had created utter devastation around himself,
causing corruption wherever he was active.
He stood upon a high peak,
and cried out from one end of the earth to the other.
And he drew to himself all those who obeyed him,
for they did not realize he was the Evil One.

But a perfect Virgin (Wisdom) stood,
proclaiming and crying out, saying,

Grace came Swiftly

The blessings of the Creative Word swiftly overcome the Evil One, the negative power. He has created illusion and separation from God throughout his realms. Working from within, from high up in the heavenly realms, he has conjured up a mirage of reflection, transience and deceit that clouds the perception of the soul. So cunningly has he concealed Reality behind this magician's veil that souls do not realize the nature and origin of his play.

But the pure Wisdom of God, the Lord's creative Power, comes from the divine eternity, from beyond the domain of the negative power. She is pristine and subtle, clear and true. She is the messenger and purveyor of Reality. She it is who furnishes both the energy and the substance with which the Evil One weaves the beguiling patterns of diversity and change that characterize his realms. Calling from within, Wisdom speaks to every soul:

> Wisdom calls aloud in the streets,
>   she raises her voice in the public squares;
> She calls out at the street corners,
>   she delivers her message at the city gates:
>
> "You ignorant people, how much longer
>   will you cling to your ignorance?
> How much longer will mockers revel in their mocking,
>   and fools hold knowledge (of God) contemptible?
> Pay attention to my warning:
>   now I will pour out my heart to you,
>   and tell you what I have to say."

Proverbs 1:20–23, JB

"O you sons of men, return!
and you, their daughters, come!
Forsake the ways of that Corruptor,
and draw near to me.
And I will enter into you,
and will bring you out from perdition,
and make you wise in the ways of Truth.

"Be not corrupted, nor perish:
hear me, and be saved;
For I bring the grace of God to you,
and through me you will be saved,
and become blessed.
I am your armour,
and they who clothe themselves in me
will not be vanquished;
But will obtain incorruption in the new world.

"O my chosen ones, walk in me!
And I will make known my ways
to them that seek me,
and will cause them to trust in my Name."

Hallelujah.

Does not Wisdom call meanwhile?
Does not Understanding raise her voice?
On the hilltop, on the road,
    at the crossways, she takes her stand;
Beside the gates of the city,
    at the approaches to the gates, she cries aloud:

"O people! I am calling to you:
    my cry goes out to all humanity.
You ignorant ones! Study discretion;
    and you fools, come to your senses!
Listen, I have important things to tell you,
    from my lips come honest words.
My mouth proclaims the truth,
    evil is abhorrent to my lips.
All the words I say are right,
    nothing crooked is in them, nothing false,
    all straightforward to him who understands,
    honest to those who know what knowledge means.
Accept my discipline rather than silver,
    knowledge of me in preference to the finest gold.
For Wisdom is more precious than pearls,
    and nothing else is so worthy of desire."

Proverbs 8:1–11; cf. JB, NJB

Wisdom says to the soul, "Come to me; let us go back to our true home. Give up the dream and seek Reality. Admit me to your heart, and I will rescue you, and fill you with my Truth. Do not give in to wickedness; do not succumb to death. Listen! Seek God! For I am the graceful Messenger, bearing the blessings of salvation. Take me as your shield and refuge. They who do this will be victorious in the holy war: they will find immortality in the spiritual world.

"You, who are so destined, take me as your companion! And I will show you paths of which you never dreamed. Those who seek my friendship will know that they can trust my hidden Name."

Ode 34

The odist observes that the spiritual path is not difficult for those who are simple, pure, wise and harmonious! Whatever is below, he says, is reflected from above. But grace is at hand to grant salvation to those who steadfastly pursue the path to eternal life.

The Way is not hard to a simple heart,
nor is there any hurdle to upright thoughts,
nor any storm in the depths of an enlightened mind.
When supported on all sides by the harmonious,
then there is no discord within.

The likeness of that which is below,
is that which is above.
For everything is from above,
and whatever is below exists only in the imagination
of those who are without Knowledge.

Grace has been revealed for your salvation:
have faith, and live and be saved.

Hallelujah.

The Way is not Hard

The mystic path is easy if the mind is still and simple; it presents no hindrance to pure thoughts. Those who see the inner light know no disturbance in themselves. Those who are filled with Truth and harmony, are always at peace within.

"As above, so below." Everything lower emanates from the higher; all things are ultimately the projection of the Divine. Physical existence forms as the material expression of the minds of all who dwell here. We are all its shareholders and its co-creators. We have jointly thought the world into existence.

It is a vast magician's show in which we are the unwitting players. But supreme blessings are at hand to bring about deliverance. Move on, then, in confidence. Live life in the Spirit; seek eternity; and go to your salvation.

Ode 35

In a rhythmic and lyrical manner, the odist describes the over-whelming, yet utterly peaceful, experience of contact with the Dew or Living Water of the Creative Word. It is, he says, his spiritual nourishment and protection. It has lifted him to the heavenly realms and taken him to his salvation.

The ode employs a wordplay in the Syriac that cannot be translated. The words "came upon", "shelter" and "dew" all possess a common root. The word used for "child" is also similar, phonetically.

Gentle showers of the Lord came upon me, granting rest,
and He caused a cloud of peace to hang above my head,
which protected me at all times,
and became the source of my salvation.

Though all things were shaken and afraid,
smoke and judgment rising from them,
I was at peace in the Word of the Lord.

More than shelter was He to me,
and more than a foundation.
I was carried like a child by his mother,
and He gave me milk, the Dew of the Lord.

And I grew strong through His gift,
and rested in His perfection.
And I spread out my hands in the ascent of my soul,
and turned myself towards the Most High,
and was redeemed by Him.

Hallelujah.

The Dew of the Lord

A soft, sweet rain of grace from heaven fell upon my soul, enfolding me in peace and bliss:

> (God) evoked clouds of brightness,
>   dropping down Dew and Life.
>
> *Psalms of Thomas I, Manichaean Psalm Book, MPB p.203*

He wrapped me in his presence, sustained my every moment, and brought about my liberation:

> Yahweh is my strength, my song,
>   he is my salvation.
> And you will draw water joyfully
>   from the Springs of salvation.
>
> *Isaiah 12:2–3, JB*

And, while I took my rest in the bliss of God's Word, the unheeding world continued on its way – the land of misery, disturbance and harsh judgment.

He was more to me than refuge, more than a dependable rock. He nurtured and held me like a mother holds her child. He fed me divine milk, the divine Dew – the Living Water – of the Lord:

> Do you not see the food of the soul, what it is? It is the *Logos* of God, raining continuously like dew, embracing all the soul, suffering no portion to be without part of itself.
>
> *Philo, Allegorical Interpretation III:59; cf. PCW1 pp.414–15, TGH1 p.247*

> Wash us now therefore in the dewdrops of your joy....
> Open to us the vaults of the heavens
>   and walk before us to the joy of your kingdom,
> O Glorious One!
>
> *Manichaean Psalm Book CCXL; cf. MPB p.41*

He will appear to you ... with a face full of joy,
    he will wash you also
    and purify you with his pleasant dews.
He will set your foot on the path of Truth
    and furnish you with your wings of light.
Manichaean Psalm Book CCLXXIX; cf. MPB p.100

And my soul expanded, was made perfect through the gift of his Word, and I found peace:

Even the dead shall arise,
    nurtured by the dew of light.
Isaiah 26:19 [8]

My heart blossomed, and my soul ascended to the heavenly realms. I turned to face my God, and he welcomed my return.

Ode 36

A description in the first person of the soul's ascent to God through the power of the Holy Spirit. Though still in human form, the soul becomes a true son of God, glorious and mighty, full of divine light and life, perfect like God, close to Him, flowing like a spring with the eternal grace of the Living Water. It is by the Lord's design, concludes the odist, that his soul has come into contact with the Spirit.

It is possible that the Saviour is speaking in part of this ode, perhaps throughout. Much depends upon whether "the shining one, the son of God" is regarded as the soul or Saviour.

I rested in the Spirit of the Lord,
and she (the Spirit) raised me to the Height;
And made me stand on my feet in the Lord's high place,
before His perfection and His glory;
And I continued praising Him
in the composition of His odes.

And she brought me before the face of the Lord,
and although I was a son of man,
I was called the shining one, the son of God.
And I was the most glorified among the glorious ones,
and the mightiest among the mighty ones.

For according to the greatness of the Most High,
so she made me.
And according to His newness (or 'gladness'),
He renewed me (or 'He made me glad').
And He anointed me with His perfection,
and I became one of those who are near to Him.
And my mouth was opened like a cloud of dew,
and my heart poured forth like a spring of holiness.
And my approach to Him was in peace,
and by His providence I was established in the Spirit.

Hallelujah.

In the Spirit of the Lord

I made my home in the Spirit of Holiness, and she carried me up to God's high realm. She took me into his eternity, and placed me before his pure resplendence; and the divine Song rang through my soul.

The Spirit enabled me to see my God. And though still living as a human being, I was transformed into a being of light, and became his son:

> As many as received him, to them gave he power
> to become the sons of God.
>
> *John 1:12, KJV*

Higher and more effulgent than the angels, mightier than the rulers – my soul was lost and found in him.

For the Spirit took me to the uttermost reaches of his Majesty, and he refreshed me with the eternal springtime of his Being. He infused me with his purity; he drew me in to him. My whole heart and soul were immersed in him, and the waters of his grace flowed through me:

> Purify me, my Bridegroom, my Saviour,
> with your Waters … that are full of grace.
>
> *Manichaean Psalm Book CCLXIII; cf. MPB p.79*

I came to him in peace; and by the good fortune of his favour, I made my home in the Spirit of Holiness.

Ode 37

A simple ode describing the divine nostalgia of the soul for God, and His response. The odist says that when the Lord heard the longing of his heart, He sent the Creative Word to him, crowning his endeavours with victory. His soul then experienced the blissful peace of eternity.

I stretched out my hands to my Lord,
and to the Most High, I raised my voice.
And I spoke with the lips of my heart,
and when my voice reached Him, He heard me.
And His Word came to me,
and gave me the fruits of my labours;
And gave me rest by the grace of the Lord.

Hallelujah.

With the Lips of my Heart

My soul yearned to be with God; divine longing made its home within me. And my heart opened to his love, calling out silently to him.

And he heard, and sent his Word, and all my efforts were rewarded. And I was blessed with the undying peace of God.

> It is ... fitting to pray to the Father
> and to call on him with all our soul –
> not externally with the lips,
> but with the spirit, which is inward.
>
> *Expository Treatise on the Soul 135, NHS21 pp.160–63*

> Pray to your Father who is in secret;
> And your Father who sees in secret
> will reward you openly.
>
> *Matthew 6:6; cf. KJV*

The odist describes his journey to eternity, having Truth – the Creative Word – as his chariot, his driver and his companion. The vicissitudes and temptations of material life are the hazards of the road. But he is never in danger, for Truth is a match for all eventualities, even those of the arch enemy, Error or Illusion – the bride or consort of the devil.

On his inner journey, he even sees the devil or negative power engaged with his companion in spinning the web of deceit and illusion, which is called the world. They invite everyone to their party, make them drunk with materiality, and rob them of their innate spiritual wealth.

But the traveller is given spiritual wisdom to keep him safe from harm. Truth gives him the strength to pass by all allurements and finally attain salvation.

I went up into the Light of Truth,
as if into a chariot;
And Truth took me,
and led me;
And carried me across hollows and gulfs,
and saved me from cliffs and floods;
And became for me a haven of salvation,
and established me in the arms of deathless life.

And he was with me and gave me rest,
and did not let me err,
because he was and is the Truth.
And I ran no risk, because I walked with him (Truth),
and I erred in nothing, because I obeyed him.
For Error fled from him,
and could never meet him;
(For Error runs a crooked race),
while Truth travels a straight path.

Truth Took me and Led me

I was drawn up on a beam of radiance, which is Truth, as if journeying in a chariot of light. Truth was my friend and guide, and he steered me on through rocky places, past chasms that yawned like death, over flood lands and quicksands that engulf the unwary. He was my safe haven; he led me into the eternal sanctuary, and gave me immortality.

Truth was my companion, and he brought me peace. He never let me stray, for he is straight and true. Nor was there ever any danger, for he was always there, and I followed him implicitly:

> He shall be a companion for you in the fearful way,
>   and he shall guide you to his kingdom,
>   and shall bring you to eternal life,
>   giving you that confidence
>   that neither passes away nor changes.
>
> *Acts of Thomas 103; cf. ANT p.409*

For Illusion and Deception can never come before him face to face, but slink away, following a crooked path.

And whatever failed my comprehension,
Truth made clear to me –
Even all the poisons of Error
and the attractions that lead to death,
which are considered to be sweetness.

And I saw the Corruptor of all that is corrupt,
even the bridegroom who corrupts and is corrupted,
while the bride who corrupts was adorning herself.
And I asked Truth, "Who are these?"

And he said to me,
"This is the Deceiver and she is Error,
and they imitate the Beloved and His bride.
And they lead the world astray,
and corrupt it.
They invite many to a banquet,
and give them to drink of their intoxicating wine.
And they cause them to vomit up their wisdom
and their understanding, rendering them witless.
And then they abandon them,
and they (the drunken ones) go about corrupted,
and like madmen.
For they have lost all understanding,
  . neither do they seek it."

But I was made wise,
so as not to fall into the hands of the Deceiver.
And I was glad
that Truth travelled with me,
For I was made strong,
and lived and was saved.

(Hallelujah!)

Whatever was beyond my understanding, he revealed to me – even the sources of Illusion and the miseries of this world of death, which people take to be sweet pleasures.

I saw the negative force responsible for all diversity and change, all birth and death – he who is the source and origin of mind and matter. With him was a companion, making herself attractive and beguiling. And I asked Truth who they were, and he replied, "This is the architect of all deception, and his companion is Illusion. Between them they lead every soul astray, taking them far from God into the labyrinth of birth and death.

"They hold continuous festival, to which all souls receive an invitation by virtue of their human birth. And they ply them with the intoxicating drink and heavy food of worldliness and sensuality. By means of it they rob them of their reason, their discrimination and their spiritual perception, and then they leave them like drunken halfwits. They drag them down into the pit of filth, and then they leave them to their own devices. And those drunken ones behave like lunatics, for they have lost all comprehension of Reality, nor do they even know It to exist":

> I stood in the midst of the world
> and in the flesh was I seen of them;
> And I found all men drunken,
> and none found I athirst (for God) among them;
> And my soul grieves over the sons of men,
> because they are blind in their heart, and see not.
> For empty they came into the world,
> and empty too they seek to leave the world.
> But for the moment they are intoxicated.
> When they shake off their wine, then they will repent.
> *Gospel of Thomas 28; cf. NHS20 pp.64–65, OLAG p.5*

But Truth held me firmly, and gave me such understanding that I could not be seduced by the deception of that powerful one. I was full of joy, because of my companion, Truth. He made me strong, and I saw through the mirage of deception that danced before my eyes. I attained to deathless life, and discovered my salvation.

Ode 38b

In a beautiful simile, the odist sees himself as a tree planted by God with His Right Hand – a metaphor for initiation or baptism into the divine Creative Word. Like a good gardener, the ground is prepared and the tree is properly planted. It grows tall, reaches maturity, and yields the fruit of salvation. But the odist gives all credit to the Lord for His skill as a planter – even for the existence of such a planting.

In the two extant Syriac manuscripts, this ode is actually placed as the ending to the previous one. Yet it stands more comfortably on its own, the imagery being quite different.

My foundations were laid by the Hand of the Lord,
for He planted me.
He dug in the root and watered it,
and made it firm and blessed it,
and its fruits will be forever.

And it rooted deeply, and sprang up tall
and spread out its branches,
and became fully grown.

And the Lord alone is to be praised for His planting,
and for His skill in cultivation:
For His care, for the blessing of His lips,
for the beautiful planting made by His Right Hand –
And for the existence of His planting,
and for the Thought of His Mind.

Hallelujah.

He Planted me

I am a tree, planted by God with his own Right Hand, with his creative Power. He tilled the ground; he buried the root; he watered it in; he firmed the ground; he gave it his blessings; and it yielded the fruit of eternity.

It put down deep roots; it rose up to the sky; it spread out great branches; and it reached maturity.

He opened my heart; he planted his Word by mystic baptism; he fed it with love; he secured it with faith; he showered it with water from his Living Spring; and he blessed my soul.

And his planting was successful: I rose to the heavens; my soul expanded and reached perfection:

> (As for) the glory of those ... who have planted in their heart the root of Wisdom, ... their face shall be turned into the light of their beauty, that they may be able to acquire and receive that world which does not die.
>
> *Apocalypse of Baruch LI:3, AB p.68*

But to the Lord alone is the credit due. His is the love, his the knowledge, his the Wisdom, his the grace. With his Right Hand, he has planted many a tree. His skill and experience are beyond comprehension, for from his divine Thought, he has devised this planting:

> He (Christ) is good. He knows his plantings,
>   because it is he who planted them in his paradise.
>
> *Gospel of Truth 36, NHS22 pp.108–9*

And, by this planting, has my soul grown up to him.

Ode 39

In a powerful image, the odist likens the Creative Word to a river in spate. Those who fight the flood – those who reject God – are swept away. Only those fearless ones, at one with the torrent, can ride it. They utilize its strength, while others are destroyed by it. For the faithful ones, the river of the Word is God's insignia with which He has marked them. They come to know His mystic Name, and they live by the strength of His Word.

Pointing to the mystic meaning behind the gospel tradition of Jesus' walking on the water, the odist continues by describing the path of the Word as an eternal bridge across the tempests of creation. It is upon these waters that the Saviour walked, his footsteps marking out a changeless and eternal path to God. This Way still exists, concludes the odist, for those who follow in his footsteps.

Like mighty rivers is the Power of the Lord,
which carry headlong those who reject Him –
And twist their footsteps,
and sweep away their crossings,
and carry off their bodies,
and corrupt their hearts.
For swifter they are than lightning,
and faster.

But those who cross in faith
shall not be shaken.
And those who walk on them in purity
shall not be afraid.
For the Sign of the Lord
is on them;
And the Sign becomes the Way
for those who cross in the Name of the Lord.

Like Mighty Rivers

More potent than a raging torrent is the Word of God, for this is the Power that energizes all creation. But those who reject God are swept away by it. Their ways become crooked, and they have no peace of mind. They fall victim to the maelstrom of incessant change, and are led towards spiritual death and ruin. For all movement in creation derives its power from this Power:

> The impetuous rush of the divine Word, borne along swiftly and ceaselessly with its strong and ordered current, overflows and gladdens the whole universe through and through.
>
> *Philo, On Dreams II:37, PCW5 pp.552–55*

> His Power, penetrating the whole of the cosmos, moves the sun and moon and turns the whole of the heavens, and is the cause of sustenance for the things of the earth.
>
> *Pseudo-Aristotle, On the Cosmos 6:398; cf. SCC p.391*

> You have created the earth by your Power
>   and the seas and deeps [by your Might].
> You have fashioned all their inhabitants
>   according to your Wisdom;
> And have appointed all that is in them,
>   according to your will.
>
> *Thanksgiving Hymns IX:10–15 (6); cf. CDSS p.253*

Those who understand and know this Power, find it their strength and refuge. Those who approach it in purity of heart are fearless of its force, since it is God's signature on all things, and he has placed His mark upon them. His Word becomes their Path, and they come to know the sweetness of His mystic Name.

Be clothed, therefore, in the Name of the Most High,
and know Him;
And you will cross without danger,
for the rivers will be subject to you.

For the Lord (Messiah) has bridged them by his Word:
he has walked over and crossed them on foot.
And his footsteps remain upon the waters,
and have not disappeared,
but are like a tree
that is firmly fixed (or 'founded on truth').
On this side and on that,
the waves rise up;
But the footsteps of our Lord Messiah remain,
and are neither obliterated nor effaced.

For a Way has been established
for those who cross after him,
and for those who follow in the footsteps of his faith,
and who adore his Holy Name.

Hallelujah.

So put on the garment of his Name, and you will discover God:

> The Name of the Lord is a strong tower:
> the righteous (man) runs into it, and is safe.
> *Proverbs 18:10; cf. KJV*

Then the flood water will hold no terrors for you, because its strength will have become your strength.

The Saviour has made a bridge out of the Word whereby to cross the stormy waters of creation. He has walked safely on its tempestuous seas:

> Guide for me my spirit
> in the midst of the stormy sea.
> *Manichaean Psalm Book, MPB p.150*

Like a tree that spans a turbulent flood, his footsteps have formed a Path to God. Though the waters rage on every side, his Tree of Life spans the torrent. It is an eternally established Path, providing a safe haven from all harm:

> O skilful Shipmaster,
> you who have conquered the raging sea:
> Your glorious Tree has come to the Harbour of Life.
> *Ephraim Syrus, ESHS4 601:15; cf. MEM p.98*

He has laid out a Highway, and those who tread it faithfully will come to know his hidden Name, and find their way to God:

> Lo, my ship I have brought to the shore;
> no storm has overwhelmed it, no wave has seized it....
> I was heading for shipwreck
> before I found the ship of Truth;
> A divine tacking was Jesus who helped me....
> An unspeakable grace overtook me.
> *Manichaean Psalm Book CCLIII, MPB p.63*

Ode 40

The odist describes the sweetness and ecstasy of his love for God. He is full with joy and gladness; his soul shines. Such souls, he concludes, will realize their essential immortality.

As honey drips from the honeycomb of bees,
and milk flows from the woman who loves her children,
so too is my hope in Thee, my God.
As water pours out from a spring,
so the praise of the Lord pours out from my heart,
and my lips utter praise to Him.

My tongue becomes sweet in His intimate converse,
and my heart expands in His psalms.⁹
My face rejoices in His gladness,
my spirit delights in His love,
and my soul shines in Him.

He who has reverence will trust in Him,
and his redemption will be assured.
His inheritance is deathless life,
and those who share in it are incorruptible.

Hallelujah.

As Honey from the Comb

Sweeter than honey, dear Lord, is my love for you. As freely as mother's milk does it flow from my yearning heart. Like water from a fountain springs the thankfulness of my soul to God:

> Better your love than life itself;
> My lips will recite your praise;
> All my life I will bless you,
>   in your name lift up my hands;
> My soul will feast most richly,
>   on my lips a song of joy and, in my mouth, praise.
>
> *Psalms 63:3–5; cf. JB, NJB*

Every part of my being is rapt with the Song of Sweetness and grows in inner holiness. Communion with the music of his Word is my delight:

> Wondrous is his Voice,
>   and his Converse otherworldly.
>
> *Mandaean Prayer Book 169, CPM p.147*

> His conversation is sweetness itself,
>   he is altogether lovable.
>
> *Song of Songs 5:16, NJB*

My face reflects my ecstasy; my heart revels in his love; my soul is radiant with his light.

He who knows such adoration will have full confidence in the Divine, and salvation will be his. His lot will be the bliss of eternity, and those who have a part in it will pass beyond the realms of time.

Ode 41

An ode of praise to the Lord for His love, His grace, His Word, and for His Saviour. The odist exhorts all God's children to worship Him; to live in His love and to be examples of all He is. The soul is eternal and has been a part of Him from the beginning; but now God has remembered the soul, says the odist, and the time has come for the soul to be reunited with Him through His pre-existent Word. This is the soul's true guide, the real Saviour who has become man, for the sake of man, to take souls back to God.

It is possible that, in the third stanza, the Saviour is speaking, its opening lines being reminiscent of passages spoken by the Saviour in *Odes 17* and *28*. Nevertheless, it seems more reasonable from the context of the present ode that it is the same voice throughout – and this is how it has been interpreted.

Let all the Lord's children praise Him,
and let us receive the truth of His faith.
His children will be acknowledged by Him:
therefore, let us sing in His love.
We live in the Lord by His grace,
and eternal Life we receive from His Messiah.

For a great day has shone upon us,
and marvellous is He who has given us His glory.
Let us all, therefore, be united in the Name of the Lord,
and let us honour Him in His goodness.
Let our faces shine in His light,
and let our hearts meditate in His love,
by night and by day:
Let us be joyful in the joy of the Lord.

All the Lord's Children

If we, in whom God has planted his Word, can truly love him, then we will experience the reality that underlies our faith. Then God will accept us. If – immersed in his love – we can listen to the divine Song, then by his blessings, our souls will come to dwell in God, and the gift of deathless Life will be granted to us by his Saviour.

For now our good times have come: his radiance has brightened up our days; we have received his sublime magnificence. We will all become one in his great Power. So let us be grateful for his kindness; let us be examples of his light:

> You are the light of the world....
> Let your light so shine before men,
>> that they may see your good works,
>> and glorify your Father who is in heaven.
>>>> *Matthew 5:14, 16; cf. KJV*

Let us meditate in his love every moment of our lives:

> Happy the man ... who meditates on his Law day and night.
>>>> *Psalms 1:1–2, JB*

Let us dance within ourselves in divine bliss and ecstasy:

> Yahweh, you have given more joy to my heart
>> than others ever knew,
>> for all their corn and wine.
>>>> *Psalms 4:7, JB*

> You have turned my mourning into dancing;
> You have stripped off my sackcloth (body)
>> and clothed me with joy;
> Now my heart will sing to you unceasingly;
> Yahweh, my God, I shall praise you forever.
>>>> *Psalms 30:11–12; cf. NJB*

All those who see me will marvel,
because I am of another race.
For the Father of Truth remembered me –
He who possessed me from the beginning.
For from His treasure was I born,
and the Thought of His heart.

And His Word is with us all along our way:
The Saviour who gives life
does not reject our souls.
The Man who humbled himself
was exalted by his own holiness:
The Son of the Most High appeared
in the perfection of His Father.

And light dawned from the Word
that was before time in Him.
And the Messiah is truly one,
and he was known before the foundation of the world;
That he might save souls forever
by the Truth of His Name.

Let a new song arise from those who love Him.

Hallelujah.

Those who know me, wonder; to them it seems as if I were from some other country, for I do not belong in this world any more:

> I listened to your words, I walked in your laws,
>   I became a stranger in the world
>   for your name's sake, my God.
>
> *Manichaean Psalm Book CCLI; cf. MPB p.60*

But God has remembered me – he whose child I have always been. For my soul is a jewel from his eternal treasury, sprung into existence by the power of his Thought – his Creative Word.

This Word is our Path; it is our companion, comforter and Saviour. The Redeemer is always with us, never turning us aside. Our Master has stooped to become man, but his holiness has not been diminished. God's primal Son, his Word, has taken birth as a man, never losing his perfection.

Through the Word is revealed the light that has always been with God. The real Saviour is this one Power that has always been with the Divine. This is the eternal Saviour who is forever carrying souls to God by the mystic Reality of his secret Holy Name.

So let us, his loving children, learn to sing this new Song that has come into our lives.

Ode 42

The concluding ode relates the traditional Christian belief that Jesus descended into hell, releasing the souls who were bound there. But the ode has a double meaning. The odist is indicating that the hell to which Jesus descended to rescue captive souls was this world, not one of the nether regions.

The odist begins by speaking of his living death on the Cross or Tree of Life, as in *Ode 27*. The Saviour then takes over, describing his coming to this world. He has come to give life and love to those who have faith in him. He enters this world – the realm of death – collects his chosen souls, and opens the inner door for them to escape into the heavenly regions. He baptizes them with the mystic Name or Word, and sets them free.

I spread out my hands, and drew near my Lord,
for the stretching out of my hands is his sign.
And my spreading out
is the outspread tree (or 'the upright cross'),
which was set up on the Way of the Righteous One.

(THE SAVIOUR:)

And I seemed to be of no account
to those who knew me;
So that I could remain hidden
from those who had no part in me,
and could be with those who love me.

All my persecutors are dead.
They who had faith in me
sought me because I was living.
And I arose and am with them,
and I will speak by their mouths.

The Living among the Dead

I took up my cross and approached my Lord. For this emblem is the Tree of Life, the Way of the Word, that reaches up to the Divine. It is the Cross of Life on which all who yearn to live must learn to die while living.

(THE SAVIOUR:) By design, I made myself seem undistinguished to the many, so that they would never guess who I really am. It left me free to care for those who recognize and love me.

My detractors in this world are all dead – spiritually. My children seek me because I have eternal life within me. I overcame the death of this world, and am always with them in my spiritual form. Now they live and speak through me.

My children have thrown off the yoke of human imperfection, and I have placed a yoke of love upon them – a gentle yoke, like the hand of the Beloved on the lover:

> Take my yoke upon you, and learn of me:
> For I am meek and lowly in heart,
>   and you shall find rest for your souls.
> For my yoke is easy, and my burden is light.
>
> *Matthew 11:29–30; cf. KJV*

Mystic union of the lover and Beloved in the heavenly realms is the way I love my children.

I was not discarded though many thought it so. I did not die as they had hoped. When I came into this world, the lord of death had been dismayed. I had come into the darkest region of creation to release souls from his grip, and he would have prevented it, could he have done so. But he could neither hold the souls (the "feet"), nor myself (the "head"), for my radiance and strength were more than his:

For they rejected those who were persecuting them,
when I laid upon them the yoke of my love:
But as the arm of the bridegroom upon the bride,
so is my yoke upon those who know me.
And as the bed that is spread in the bridal chamber,
so is my love for those who believe in me.

And I was not rejected,
though I was reckoned to be so.
And I did not perish,
though they supposed it of me.

Sheol saw me, and was troubled:
Death disgorged me and many with me.
I was gall and bitterness to him,
and I went down with him to his lowest depth.
And he let go of the feet and the head,
because he was unable to endure my face.

And I made an assembly of the living among his dead,
and I spoke to them with living lips,
so that my Word should not be without effect.
And those who had died ran to me,
and they cried out, saying,
"Have pity on us, Son of God,
and deal with us according to thy kindness,
and bring us out of the bonds of darkness.
And open for us the door,
that by it we may go forth to thee,
for we perceive that death does not touch thee.
Let us also be saved by thee,
for thou art our Saviour."

You descended into Sheol with mighty power,
    and the dead saw you and became alive,
    and the lord of death was not able to bear it;
And you ascended with great glory,
    and you took up with you
    all who sought refuge with you;
And marked out for them the Path leading up on high,
    and in your footsteps all your redeemed followed.

Acts of Thomas 8; cf. AAA p.288

So I gathered my family of souls around me, here in the prison of death. I initiated them into my Word, breathing spiritual life into them. They understood my message, and their yearning hearts called out, "You are kind and merciful. Have compassion and release us from this dark prison. Open the door to the inner heavens, so that we may escape this body and meet with you within. Bless us with the salvation that is yours to give":

Save me from an evil death!
Bring me from a tomb alive....
Save me from sinful flesh,
    because I trusted in you with all my strength!
Because you are the life of the life,
    save me from a humiliating Enemy!
Do not give me into the hand of a Judge
    who is severe with sin!

Second Apocalypse of James 63, NHS11 pp.146–47

And I heard their voices,
and I treasured their faith in my heart,
and I sealed my Name upon their foreheads.
For they are free (or 'noble') men,
and they are mine.

Hallelujah.

And their yearning touched my heart. I accepted their love; I kept it safe in my heart; and I baptized them with the mystic Name. And now they are true holy men, and free, for they are my special children:

> The hour is coming, and now is,
>   when the dead shall hear the Voice of the Son of God:
> And they that hear shall live.

John 5:25, KJV

NOTES AND REFERENCES

1. A Sufi mystic – but the source of this extract has proved elusive!
2. *Aeon* is a very common gnostic term with a wide spread of meaning. Sometimes translated as 'worlds', sometimes as 'powers', *aeon* is a Greek word conveying the idea of something vast. Often, it is left untranslated since its meaning is difficult to convey by just one English word. *Aeons* are both the inner realms and the ruling power behind them.
3. See note 2.
4. Although, according to the setting in John's gospel, these words are attributed to Jesus, they are actually those of the unknown gospel writer himself, writing in the name of the Word, just like the authors of the Wisdom literature. As many biblical scholars have pointed out, John's gospel is really an extended allegorical discourse on the Word or *Logos,* using the gospel story as a framework.
5. *Cf. Genesis* 2:7, 6:17, 7:15, 7:22.
6. See *Gospel of Jesus, GJ* index: Only-Begotten.
7. *Matthew* 3:13–17.
8. Translation from an unpublished lecture by Rabbi Jerry Steinberg, in *HN* p.115.
9. *Lit.* "my members grow fat in his psalms."

ABBREVIATIONS

See *Bibliography* for full details.

AAA	*Apocryphal Acts of the Apostles,* W.R. Wright
AB	*Apocalypse of Baruch,* tr. R.H. Charles
AF1–2	*The Apostolic Fathers,* 2 vols., tr. Kirsopp Lake
ANT	*The Apocryphal New Testament,* M.R. James
AOT	*The Apocryphal Old Testament,* ed. H.E.D. Sparks
BCB	*Breviarium Chaldaicum,* 3 vols., P. Bedjan
BD	*The Book of the Dove,* Bar Hebraeus, tr. A.J. Wensinck
CDSS	*The Complete Dead Sea Scrolls in English,* tr. G. Vermes
CH	*The Clementine Homilies,* tr. Thomas Smith *et al.*
CPM	*The Canonical Prayerbook of the Mandaeans,* tr. E.S. Drower
ESHS	*Sancti Ephraemi Syri Hymni et Sermones,* 4 vols., T.J. Lamy
FFF	*Fragments of a Faith Forgotten,* G.R.S. Mead
HN	*The Holy Name: Mysticism in Judaism,* Miriam Caravella
JB	*The Jerusalem Bible* (1966)
KJV	*The Holy Bible: Authorized King James Version*
MAA	"Mythological Acts of the Apostles", A.S. Lewis
MBB	*Ein Manichäisches Bet- und Beichtbuch,* W.B. Henning
MEM	*Mesopotamian Elements in Manichaeism,* G. Widengren
ML	*Manichaean Literature,* J.P. Asmussen
MM1–3	"Mitteliranische Manichaica aus Chinesisch-Turkestan", 3 vols., F.C. Andreas and W.B. Henning
MPB	*A Manichaean Psalm-Book,* Part II, ed. & tr. C.R.C. Allberry
NHS11	*Nag Hammadi Studies* XI: *Nag Hammadi Codices V,2–5 and VI,* ed. D.M. Parrott
NHS20	*Nag Hammadi Studies* XX: *Nag Hammadi Codex II,2–7,* vol. 1, ed. B. Layton
NHS21	*Nag Hammadi Studies* XXI: *Nag Hammadi Codex II, 2–7,* vol. 2, ed. B. Layton

NHS22   *Nag Hammadi Studies* XXII: *Nag Hammadi Codex* I *(the Jung Codex)*, 2 vols., ed. H.W. Attridge

NHS28   *Nag Hammadi Studies* XXVIII: *Nag Hammadi Codices XI, XII, XIII*, ed. C.W. Hedrick

NHS30   *Nag Hammadi Studies* XXX: *Nag Hammadi Codex VII, XIII*, ed. Birger A. Pearson

NIV   *The Holy Bible: New International Version* (1973)

NJB   *The New Jerusalem Bible* (1985)

NJPS   *Tanakh: The Holy Scriptures*, The New Jewish Publication Society translation (1988)

NR1–2   *The Nestorians and Their Rituals*, 2 vols., G.P. Badger

NRSV   *The Holy Bible: New Revised Standard Version* (1989)

OLAG   *The Oxyrhynchus Logia and the Apocryphal Gospels*, C. Taylor

OPJG   *The Origin of the Prologue to St John's Gospel*, J.R. Harris

OPS   *The Odes and Psalms of Solomon*, tr. J.R. Harris and A. Mingana (1920)

PCW1–10 *Philo*, 10 vols., tr. F.H. Colson and G.H. Whitaker

PNC   *A Pair of Nasoraean Commentaries*, tr. E.S. Drower

PS   *Pistis Sophia*, tr. V. MacDermot

PSW   *The Prodigal Soul: The Wisdom of Ancient Parables*, John Davidson

RSV   *The Holy Bible: Revised Standard Version* (1952)

SCMP   *Studies in the Coptic Manichaean Psalm-Book*, T. Säve-Söderbergh

SCC   *On Sophistical Refutations, On Coming-to-Be and Passing-Away, and On the Cosmos*, Aristotle, tr. E.M. Forster and D.J. Furley

SSM1–3   *Studies of the Spanish Mystics*, 3 vols., E.A. Peers

TGH1–3   *Thrice-Greatest Hermes*, 3 vols., G.R.S. Mead

TTQ   *The Thousand and Twelve Questions (Alf Trisar Shuialia)*, tr. E.S. Drower

TYN   *The New Testament*, tr. William Tyndale

WCA1–2   *The Writings of Clement of Alexandria*, 2 vols., tr. W. Wilson

BIBLIOGRAPHY

Those books used or quoted in the text are included, together with a few others of particular interest. Subsections include both primary sources as well as studies, commentaries and so on. Editions referenced in the text are the ones listed below. Dates of first publication have been added in square brackets where significant. Books and articles are listed by their title, rather than by author or translator – in a selection such as this, it makes them easier to find. For a more complete bibliography of early Christian studies, see *The Gospel of Jesus: In Search of His Original Teachings* (John Davidson, 1995, rev. edn. 2004).

Bibles

The Holy Bible: Authorized King James Version [1611]; Oxford University Press, Oxford.

The Holy Bible: New International Version; Hodder and Stoughton, London, 1973.

The Holy Bible: New Revised Standard Version; Oxford University Press, New York, 1989.

The Holy Bible: Revised Standard Version; Oxford University Press, Oxford, 1952.

The Holy Scriptures; Jewish Publication Society, Philadelphia, 1955.

The Jerusalem Bible; Darton, Longman and Todd, London, 1966.

The New Jerusalem Bible; Darton, Longman and Todd, London, 1985.

The New Testament: The Text of the Worms Edition of 1526 in Original Spelling, tr. William Tyndale, ed. W.R. Cooper; British Library, 2000 [1526].

Tanakh: The Holy Scriptures, The New Jewish Publication Society translation; Jewish Publication, Philadelphia, 1988.

Early Christian, Gnostic and Jewish Literature

Apocalypse of Baruch, tr. R.H. Charles; SPCK, London, 1917.

The Apocryphal Acts of the Apostles, tr. W.R. Wright; Williams and Norgate, Edinburgh, 1871.

The Apocryphal New Testament, tr. M.R. James; Oxford University Press, Oxford, 1989 [1924].

The Apocryphal Old Testament, ed. H.E.D. Sparks; Oxford University Press, Oxford, 1985.

The Apostolic Fathers, 2 vols., tr. Kirsopp Lake; William Heinemann, London, 1912–13.

The Book of the Dove, Bar Hebraeus, tr. A.J. Wensinck; E.J. Brill, Leiden, 1919.

Breviarium Chaldaicum, 3 vols., P. Bedjan; Leipzig, 1886–87.

The Canonical Prayerbook of the Mandaeans, tr. E.S. Drower; E.J. Brill, Leiden, 1959.

The Clementine Homilies, tr. Thomas Smith *et al.;* T. & T. Clark, Edinburgh, 1870.

The Complete Dead Sea Scrolls in English, tr. G. Vermes; Penguin, London, 1998.

The Divine Romance: Tales of an Unearthly Love, John Davidson; Clear Books, Bath, UK, 2004.

Ein Manichäisches Bet- und Beichtbuch, W.B. Henning; Berlin, 1937; also in *Abhandlungen der Königlich Preussischen Akademie der Wissenschaften* (1936), Berlin.

Fragments of a Faith Forgotten, G.R.S. Mead; Health Research, Mokelumne Hill, California, 1976 [1906].

The Gnostic Scriptures, B. Layton; SCM, London, 1987.

The Gospel According to Thomas, tr. A. Guillaumont *et al.;* E.J. Brill, Leiden, 1959.

The Gospel of Jesus: In Search of His Original Teachings, rev. edn., John Davidson; Science of the Soul Research Centre, New Delhi, and Clear Books, Bath, UK, 2004 [1995].

The Hymns and Homilies of Ephraim the Syrian and the Demonstrations of Aphrahat the Persian Sage, tr. J. Gwynn; James Parker, Oxford, 1898.

Manichaean Literature, J.P. Asmussen; Scholars' Facsimiles and Reprints, Delmar, New York, 1975.

A Manichaean Psalm-Book, Part II, ed. & tr. C.R.C. Allberry; Kohlhammer, Stuttgart, 1938.

"Mesopotamian Elements in Manichaeism", G. Widengren; in *Uppsala Universitets Arsskrift* 3 (1946), University of Uppsala, Sweden.

"Mitteliranische Manichaica aus Chinesisch-Turkestan", 3 vols., F.C. Andreas and W.B. Henning; in *Sitzungsberichte der Königlich Preussischen Akademie der Wissenschaften* (1932, 1933, 1934), Berlin.

"The Mythological Acts of the Apostles", A.S. Lewis; in *Horae Semiticae* IV (1904); C.J. Clay, London.

The Nag Hammadi Library in English, ed. J.M. Robinson; E.J. Brill, Leiden, 1988.

Nag Hammadi Studies XI: *Nag Hammadi Codices V,2–5 and VI,* ed. Douglas M. Parrott; E.J. Brill, Leiden, 1979.

Nag Hammadi Studies XV: *Nag Hammadi Codices IX and X,* ed. Birger A. Pearson; E.J. Brill, Leiden, 1981.

Nag Hammadi Studies XX: *Nag Hammadi Codex II,2–7,* vol. 1, ed. Bentley Layton; E.J. Brill, Leiden, 1989.

Nag Hammadi Studies XXI: *Nag Hammadi Codex II,2–7,* vol. 2, ed. Bentley Layton; E.J. Brill, Leiden, 1989.

Nag Hammadi Studies XXII: *Nag Hammadi Codex I (the Jung Codex),* vol. 1, ed. Harold W. Attridge; E.J. Brill, Leiden, 1985.

Nag Hammadi Studies XXVIII: *Nag Hammadi Codices XI, XII, XIII,* ed. Charles W. Hedrick; E.J. Brill, Leiden, 1990.

The Nestorians and Their Rituals, 2 vols., G.P. Badger; Joseph Masters, London, 1852.

Nag Hammadi Studies XXX: *Nag Hammadi Codex VII, XIII,* ed. Birger A. Pearson; E.J. Brill, Leiden, 1996.

The Old Testament Pseudoepigrapha, 2 vols., ed. J.H. Charlesworth; Darton, Longman and Todd, London, 1983.

The Origin of the Prologue to St John's Gospel, J.R. Harris; Cambridge University Press, Cambridge, 1917.

The Oxyrhynchus Logia and the Apocryphal Gospels, C. Taylor; Oxford University Press, Oxford, 1899.

A Pair of Nasoraean Commentaries, tr. E.S. Drower; E.J. Brill, Leiden, 1963.

The Prodigal Soul: The Wisdom of Ancient Parables, John Davidson; Clear Books, Bath, UK, 2004.

The Robe of Glory: An Ancient Parable of the Soul, John Davidson; Element, Shaftesbury, UK, 1992.

Sancti Ephraemi Syri Hymni et Sermones, 4 vols., T.J. Lamy; Mechliniae, 1882–1902.

Select Works of St Ephrem the Syrian, tr. J.B. Morris; John Henry Parker, Oxford, 1847.

Studies in the Coptic Manichaean Psalm-Book, T. Säve-Söderbergh; Uppsala, Sweden & W. Heffer, Cambridge, 1949.

The Teachings of Silvanus, J. Zandee; Nederlands Instituut voor het Nabije Oosten, Leiden, 1991.

The Thousand and Twelve Questions (Alf Trisar Shuialia), tr. E.S. Drower; Akademie-Verlag, Berlin, 1960.

The Writings of Clement of Alexandria, 2 vols., tr. W. Wilson; T. & T. Clark, Edinburgh, 1867, 1869.

Miscellaneous

The Holy Name: Mysticism in Judaism, M.B. Caravella; Radha Soami Satsang Beas, Dera Baba Jaimal Singh, Punjab, 2000 [1989].

Luis de León: A Study of the Spanish Renaissance, A.F.G. Bell; Oxford University Press, Oxford, 1925.

On Sophistical Refutations, On Coming-to-Be and Passing-Away, and On the Cosmos, Aristotle, tr. E.M. Forster & D.J. Furley; William Heinemann, London, 1955.

Philo, 10 vols., tr. F.H. Colson and G.H. Whitaker; William Heinemann, London, 1941.

The Song of Songs: The Soul and the Divine Beloved, John Davidson; Clear Books, Bath, UK, 2004.

Studies of the Spanish Mystics, 3 vols., E.A. Peers; SPCK, London, 1951–60 [1926–60].

Thrice-Greatest Hermes, 3 vols., G.R.S. Mead; Theosophical Publishing Society, London, 1906.

A Treasury of Mystic Terms, Part I, 6 vols., ed. John Davidson; Science of the Soul Research Centre, New Delhi, 2003.

Odes of Solomon

The Odes and Psalms of Solomon, 2 vols., J.R. Harris and A. Mingana; Longmans, Green and Company, London, 1920.

The Odes and Psalms of Solomon, J.R. Harris; Cambridge University Press, Cambridge, 1911.

"The Odes of Solomon", tr. J.A. Emerton; in *The Apocryphal Old Testament*, ed. H.E.D. Sparks; Oxford University Press, Oxford, 1985.

The Odes of Solomon, tr. J.H. Bernard; Cambridge University Press, Cambridge, 1912.

"The Odes of Solomon", tr. J.H. Charlesworth; in *The Old Testament Pseudoepigrapha*, 2 vols., ed. J.H. Charlesworth; Darton, Longman and Todd, London, 1983.

The Odes of Solomon, tr. J.H. Charlesworth; Oxford University Press, Oxford, 1973.